DIARY OF A DEADHEAD

A Wild Magical Ride into the World of Sound and Vibration

CANDACE CARSON

Copyright © 2015 Candace Carson
All rights reserved.

ISBN: 151186933X
ISBN 13: 9781511869331
Library of Congress Control Number: 2015906852
CreateSpace Independent Publishing Platform
North Charleston, South Carolina

DEADHEADS

Deadheads are a tribe unto themselves. Trying to explain the higher vibrations that could be reached during a magical moment of listening to, and being part of, a piece of music being played by the Grateful Dead is really impossible, but I am going to try.

According to Wikipedia, "Deadhead" is a name given to fans of the American jam band the Grateful Dead. In the 1970s, a number of fans began traveling to see the band in as many shows or festival venues as they could. With large numbers of people thus attending strings of shows, a community developed. Deadheads developed their own idiom and slang.

There is no name, no label that can be given to explain this extraordinary journey on the road with the Grateful Dead. What could we possibly call it? The Grateful Dead captured their audience as no other band ever had—past or present. This was not something they set out to do. It just happened; it was a perfect storm. The music captivated; it was somehow different and unexpected. It drew you in, and you craved more. Not everyone caught the fever. Who knows why some did and some did not? You could not explain it to those who did not fall victim to the sound. Being a Deadhead was a wild, magical ride into the world of color and sound and vibration. The music led us to a oneness and to a connection with each other, where we immersed ourselves in the childlike joy of the heart. In the vortex of the music, we connected to one another and to the unseen energy of sound. It was a moment in which we could step out of time and space and experience a different reality. It was a crazy trip that none of us could have imagined or predicted. We just jumped on the train and took the magical ride into the dream world of our own making.

Many books have been written about the Grateful Dead, the band members, and their journeys and experiences. I am writing this book from the outer circle, from the perspective of a dedicated fan of the Grateful Dead, a Deadhead. The songs and the music influenced the very fabric of my life and became my spiritual journey. My choices, my relationships, and my quest for knowledge and understanding of my inner being became my voyage. Dancing with the Grateful Dead, my body, mind, and spirit found the elusive vibration of oneness. In the music I found present-moment awareness, and here I entered the now. I became one with the music and found my connection to source, God, the universe, or whatever name you wish to give it.

I have never had a conversation with another Deadhead about how this experience is a spiritual journey, but I do believe most Deadheads would agree with me that what we experienced was something magical, intoxicating, and very hard to explain. The music sparked the band, and the band members and the Deadheads each played their own part in this mutually intertwined theater. The Grateful Dead chose to walk the path of creating music for the misfits and freaks that followed them from town to town. We Deadheads, as their partners in this implausible endeavor, followed our hearts and connected with the music, dancing with them as one on this long, bizarre voyage called the Grateful Dead.

Rather than having an orchestrated performance, the Grateful Dead improvised, working the details of songs out in front of a live audience. Their songs were works in progress, the music forever changing. At times the music could be mind-blowing and exhilarating; at times it could be lackadaisical and erratic. The time, the place, and the atmosphere all determined the vibrations of the experience. Even if the music felt fickle or ambivalent, it did not matter. It was a roller-coaster ride filled with highs and lows, and it was the imperfection that made the experience so real and intoxicating.

The Grateful Dead's live performances became my church, my religion, and my place of worship. The music became my refuge in times of loneliness. Dancing with the Dead and being with like-minded people gave me a figurative home and brought to me an awareness of connecting to my higher self and to my fellow Deadheads. The music took me to a place I had never encountered before; it spoke to my spirit, and my soul soaked it in like a desert cactus in desperate need of refreshing, life-giving water.

Deadheads created the music with the band. We were the feedback, the other side of the coin. Reaching the highs and lows simultaneously, we rode that wave of magical bliss and utter craziness together. This was the part of the whole Grateful Dead phenomenon that the world in general did not understand; we were all the Grateful Dead.

As I embarked on this endeavor to transcribe my incredible adventures of dancing to the music of the Grateful Dead, I realized this tale was a written history of not only my own personal journey but also that of a whole generation. It dawned on me that the events that transpired in the 1960s and 1970s were not mine personally; they were ours, belonging to any child born to parents of the World War II generation. My story is a reflection of all of our lives, a story of how the music of our generation shaped our beliefs, opened the doors of allowance, and shifted into a new reality and era. We discovered and awakened new paradigms, and our concepts of truths began to change. As we danced to the new music of life, our generation asked, "Is there more?" We are all connected in this tapestry of life, all influenced by the amazing and creative musicians, artists, and authors of our time.

Chapter 1
THE CORNERS OF MY MIND

This is my tale of discovery, the story of how life led me to dance to the music of my generation, and of how I found my way to the family of the Grateful Dead.

I was born in the chilly, steel-gray winter month of November 1955, in the industrial town of Aurora, Illinois, forty miles directly west of Chicago. My father was one of ten children born to Hungarian immigrants. As a child of the Depression era, he lived most of his young life in poverty.

My mom was an orphan in Litchfield, England, until the age of seven, when she was adopted by a middle-class couple from the "Black Country" of Tipton, England. She grew up amid the bombings of World War II and spent many nights huddled with her parents in the bomb shelter in their backyard.

I was raised in a Hungarian-Romanian neighborhood, in a house right next to the one in which my father had been born and raised. The old immigrant women of the neighborhood wore babushkas, or colorful scarves wrapped around their heads, and in their broken English told their stories from the old country. They each possessed their own unique version of an authentic stuffed-cabbage recipe. They grew their own food in their backyard gardens, canned their own pickles and tomatoes, and cooked homemade meals from the recipes passed on from their mothers. The train tracks that ran through town were just two blocks from my home, and I fell asleep each night listening to the comforting whistles of the freight trains rolling down the tracks. I have two older brothers, Robin and David, and a younger sister, Cindy.

As I wound my way back through my memories to the beginning of my story, I realized my tremendous love of music, dance, and laughter was passed on from my parents. I cannot imagine a home or a life without music. Music knows no boundaries. It crosses all cultural, social, and economic lines. We can write the history of the human race through the music of each era, starting with the drumming of the cave dwellers through ever-evolving music of the twenty-first century. As children we learn to express ourselves through song, and we unleash our pent-up energy through dance. Even a two-year-old will dance to a tune, feeling that vibration of the universal language of music. As we grow older and listen to the music of our own generation, we invoke memories of the past, and major turning points in our lives are often punctuated by the music of our time. To me, music is freedom. It allows self-expression through song and dance; music speaks to my heart and to my soul and connects me to my fellow human beings. Music paints a conceptual picture of our past, engages us in the present moment, and leads our imagination to the wonderment of our future.

I was fortunate enough to be born with the awakening scene of rock and roll and the incredible music that emerged out of the 1950s, 1960s, and 1970s. Elvis opened the door of the changing direction in the world of music with his electric guitar, his sexy good looks, and his swinging hips, and my generation eagerly danced through to a new and exciting era. Our view of the world and our changing attitudes were expedited with a television in many homes. At the age of eight, I was listening to the Beatles. I was riveted to the television set watching those long-haired Brits on February 9, 1964, as they performed live on the Ed Sullivan show.

I was captivated and infatuated. I had the Beatle boots, the bobble-head dolls, the cards that came with the pink bubble gum, and all the teen magazines with the hundreds of photos of these new rock phenomena. You name it, I had it, and at the tender age of eight, I was a groupie. I begged my dad to take me into Chicago to see the Beatles live, but he wouldn't. He revealed to me in later years that he had been afraid to drive the unfamiliar city streets of Chicago. He did, however, take me and a few friends in our old blue station wagon, armed with large bags of buttered popcorn, to the drive-in theater to see *A Hard Day's Night*. Many years later, as I watched that movie again, I wondered what my dad must have thought during that scene when John Lennon puts the Coca-Cola bottle up to his nose, pretending to snort cocaine!

When I was a young child, we had a record player set in a rectangular veneer console in our living room. Mom and Dad loved music, and they loved to sing and dance. My mom has a beautiful singing voice, and when we were children, she would rock us to sleep singing the old classic nursery rhymes. She had a transistor radio in the kitchen, and with her flowered apron hung around her neck as she baked Christmas cookies, she would sing "White Christmas" along with Perry Como. In church on Sundays, she and Dad sang loudly and with much enthusiasm, as my sister and I cringed with embarrassment in the corner of the pew. At wedding receptions held in the old VFW or the Knights of Columbus hall, they danced the jitterbug to the big-band sounds of the 1940s, the dancing growing wilder as the beer flowed and the hour grew late. They knew how to party and have a good time. The apple does not fall far from the tree.

In the 1960s, at five thirty in the evening, our family of six would sit in our appointed chairs around the Formica table in our tiny kitchen eating a home-cooked meal. Unless, of course, my dad was on duty at the fire department—then Mom could get away with feeding us Swanson's frozen dinners, which we all loved! After the dishes were washed and dried, we would gather around our black-and-white television and watch our favorite TV shows. Dad loved Red Skelton, Andy Griffith, and *The Honeymooners*. *The Andy Williams Show* was Mom's favorite program, as she knew all the songs and could sing along. My brothers, Robin and David, loved the westerns: *Gunsmoke*, *The Rifleman*, and *Rawhide*, along with *Route 66* and *Dragnet*. Cindy and I preferred *The Flintstones*, *The Beverly Hillbillies*, and *Bewitched*; I always wanted to be able to twitch my nose and manifest whatever I desired or clean my room in mere seconds. In 1966 my favorite

TV show became *The Monkees,* and rock-and-roll music became an influential force in my very young life. In 1968 *Rowan & Martin's Laugh-In* captured the whole family with its wacky cast of characters and edgy sketches, which often conveyed sexual innuendo or politically charged yet humorous content.

On Saturday mornings I would tune in to Dick Clark and *American Bandstand*, where I could hear all the new music and learn a few new dance moves. At the time there were numerous musical variety shows to watch, such as *Hollywood a Go Go, Shindig!,* and *Where the Action Is*, all tantalizing our imaginations and molding this new, young teenage-hippie generation. It was the beginning of the MTV culture and the introduction of what would one day become classic rock and roll. The new music captivated and changed us all, and we didn't even need to leave our living rooms to be part of the scene or the developing times.

American life in the 1960s was exploding with shifting attitudes toward politics and social standards through the evolution of rock music and rock musicians. Jazz, blues, country, and folk music were influencing the new rock era and our changing times. Racial boundaries were expanding with the influences of the music, and our whole outlook on what was deemed normal was evolving. With the new rock music, the hippie generation emerged. The hair grew longer, the drugs got harder, and the clothes and colors exploded into a rainbow of self-expression and creativity. The musical lyrics intensified with pointed opposition to sending a generation of young men off to war and to the racial conflicts violently erupting all across the country. The songs were no longer the simplistic love songs like "I Want to Hold Your Hand"; they were exceedingly more complicated and poignant, like the Beatles "Revolution," and Crosby, Stills, Nash, and Young's "Ohio."

Psychedelic drugs were expanding minds and influencing the music, and even though I was a young teenager at the time, I knew things were morphing into something drastically different from my parents' generation. It was a bit frightening, and yet exhilarating, to be on the cusp of this new Aquarian age. Assassinations, political riots, and the killing of college students at Kent State seemed to be the norm. Jimi Hendrix woke us up and turned us on our heads by playing the national anthem with his saucy electric guitar and his on-stage sexual escapades. The music was also becoming a congruous outlet for our changing attitudes toward sexual expressions and freedoms. We were saying no to the white-bread suburban generation that fought in World War II. We were saying no to the religious dogma that was not feeding our souls. Instead of attending church, we were going to rock concerts. Woodstock conveyed to the world that the peace-loving hippies were passionate about their music and compassionate toward their causes. Change was inevitable. We were standing up and protesting the Vietnam War and the political and social injustices that were evident around our world.

CHAPTER 2
MY SOLDIER BROTHER

The Vietnam War was a confusing contrast in my impressionable young life. In June of 1965, my brother Robin, who always wanted to be a soldier, decided to join the army and fight for his country as our father had fought in World War II. He was only seventeen years old, and Dad had to sign papers giving him permission to enlist. Robin was a sweet, quiet, loving boy who could sit for hours reading a book. He enjoyed the outdoors and loved all forms of nature. I remember him toting home slimy, creepy frogs; lizards; snakes; and turtles from the rivers he loved to fish on hot and humid summer afternoons. I could not imagine him going to fight in a war where he would have to kill and witness the horrors of battle. I was frightened for him, and this idea of joining the army to become a soldier that killed other humans seemed ludicrous to me. I did not want him to go, but who was going to listen to a child? Robin is eight years my senior, yet we were very close siblings. He was my protector, my confidant, and my teacher.

Robin was the first person to introduce to me the music of country and blues. Together we would sit in the living room and listen to his forty-fives on the record player. On warm summer afternoons, we would meander our way through the neighborhoods to a white clapboard house that was the local record store. There we would peruse all the new releases. He inherited my mom's beautiful singing voice, and I can still picture him singing Marty Robins 1960s number-one hit "El Paso" shortly before he left for basic training. In later years my fondest memory of Robin singing is him driving his pickup truck on a desert highway, the windows wide open and the warm winds washing over us, and him belting out Bob Seger's "Turn the Page." He loved Roy Orbison, Roger Miller, Otis Redding, Joan Baez, and all of the other country-folk-blues singers of the late 1950s and early 1960s.

When I was a little girl and scared to sleep alone, Robin would let me crawl into bed with him, and he would conjure up whimsical stories of the little elves and fairies that lived in Mom's flower gardens. My imagination would carry me away to a magical world of tiny, invisible creatures, and I would fall asleep with sweet mystical dreams. With the day of his impending departure for the army looming over us, I was wondering who was going to snuggle with me; who was going to hold me when I was scared, ease my fear in the dark of night? The day Robin left for basic training, David, Cindy, and I stayed home from school. I don't think Mom could bear to have the house be silent when Robin walked out that door. After taking photos with our Polaroid camera of Robin and his girlfriend of that time, Dad drove him to the bus terminal. It was my first taste of emptiness.

After Robin was in the army, I remember watching the news about the Vietnam War on our black-and-white television. Dad would turn on the nightly news, and we would be glued to the television as Walter Cronkite showed pictures of the American and South Vietnamese soldiers fighting the Vietcong, along with pictures of crying children and dead bodies. I cannot imagine why my parents allowed me to watch this, but they did. What a surreal contrast between a brutal war and the warm-and-fuzzy *Donna Reed Show*. I would go to bed with those gory pictures embedded in my mind and worry about my big brother, praying for God to keep him safe.

On January 7, 1967, after only being in Vietnam for a few months, Robin stepped on a land mine and lost the lower part of his leg at the young age of nineteen. His body was pummeled with shrapnel. Of course, those were only the wounds that could be seen; the mental and emotional wounds would be his real enemy for many years to come.

Chapter 3
LOVE, THE ONLY ANSWER

I was in the seventh grade at St. Theresa Catholic School the day the first telegram arrived informing our family that Robin had been wounded. I remember walking out of school for the day and noticing my cousin Jimmy standing there, waiting to drive Cindy and me home. This was very unusual—we almost always walked home—but I did not think to question him as he spent a lot of time at our house, and I thought he was being nice. When we arrived home, all of my aunts and uncles—my dad's four brothers and five sisters and their spouses—along with a few older cousins were lingering about our kitchen. Again, this was unusual, but I was not alarmed as I knew they had all attended the funeral of an older neighbor that day. I assumed they were just visiting after the funeral services, which is what people did in those days. As I was heading up the stairs to my bedroom, my mom stopped me and said, very nonchalantly, "Robin has been wounded." No details followed, and I had no idea what "wounded" meant, but my heart sank into my stomach. The next morning my sister and I were shuffled off to school and Mass, which we always attended before school and during which the priest asked that everyone pray for Robin. I proceeded to get up, walk outside, and throw up my orange juice. Shaking and crying, I was sent home.

I was home a few days later when the day the second telegram arrived, a shiny black car pulling into the driveway and then two men in army uniforms coming up to the door to deliver information on Robin's condition.

I clearly remember my mom shakily sitting down in a little chair in our living room to open that telegram, not knowing what fate was awaiting us; it said Robin was being sent stateside for his recovery. After that second telegram arrived, life took a dramatic turn, and routines in our home became very erratic.

Robin was in Valley Forge Hospital in Pennsylvania for close to a year, and within that year my parents traveled there to visit him several times. When they traveled back east, Cindy and I would be farmed out to neighbors or relatives to be looked after; David was old enough to be left on his own. My innocence was shattered, life at home was no longer easygoing, and I became my sister's protector as Robin had been my protector. Looking after her as our family was scattered about became my unspoken responsibility. Everything now revolved around Robin's healing and then bringing him home. I felt lost and alone, and I missed my big brother. I did not understand this war in a foreign country that tore families apart. I did not understand this world I was living in, a world where presidents and people fighting for social equality were assassinated. I did not understand the tensions between the black and white races; my young twelve-year-old mind did not understand why we could not all just love each other! There were no simple answers to my questions or my confusion.

In the following years, as I grew older and life moved forward, I found myself relating more and more to music. It touched my heart and my soul, and I realized through music that I was not alone in my confusion and discontent. I had the Beatles' "All You Need Is Love," Simon and Garfunkel's "Sound of Silence," and then, in 1969, the Fifth Dimension's "Age of Aquarius" telling me something new was waiting to be born.

As a child who had been raised in the Catholic faith, I had learned to pray at a very early age and had been introduced to the idea of spirits, so praying, and later communing with unseen energies, seemed natural to me. My favorite saint to pray to when I was young was the Mother Mary, and when I prayed to her it would be for protection to keep my family safe when we traveled or to help heal someone who was ill. After Robin was wounded, my family no longer felt safe. I found no solace in praying—no comfort, no feeling of belonging to my church, and no connection to anything, for that matter. There was nowhere to turn to find comfort, and I had no idea how to express the turbulent feelings swirling about my mind and in my heart. I felt as if I were alone in a world that did not understand the turmoil my family was going through.

So I turned to my many friends, and I tuned in to the music. Through music I connected not only to my peers but also to my inner self (although at the time I could not have told you that). I did not realize that through the songs that touched my heart I was connecting to my source, to my higher being. Through music I found the comfort I was longing for.

Chapter 4
SEARCHING FOR A PATH

I navigated my way through the tumultuous times of the late 1960s and the early 1970s searching for some direction—any arrow pointing toward a path that might make sense to me—but that path eluded me.

Robin came home from the hospital right before Christmas of 1967. At the veterans' hospital, he was sewn up, given a new leg, and then sent on his way. Robin was never treated for the emotional trauma of losing a limb or for the atrocities of war that he had witnessed, and returning to family life was not an easy transition for him. He had been on morphine and pain medication for his physical wounds for a year, and when he returned home there were plenty more drugs to choose from: wicked-strong Panama Red pot to smoke and get you stoned, Quaaludes to slow you down, and white-cross speed to pick you up and get you moving again. And there was heroin. Robin found his way to every doctor in town, and they all gladly gave him some form of downer for his physical pain. No one even attempted to deal with his emotional pain and instability. It was not a big jump for him to go from his prescribed pain meds to heroin. And with the drugs, life unraveled. (As I write this in 2014, nothing has changed; our veterans still suffer tremendous psychological pain, often turning to drugs and suicide as an answer.)

At one point in the midst of this continual dysfunction that enveloped our lives, Dad and my brother David drove Robin to the VA hospital in Chicago, seeking any form of help. In utter desperation Dad was hoping to have Robin admitted to the psychiatric ward of the hospital, but without power of attorney Robin would have to agree to this plan. He did not. Robin met with the doctor first and told his tale of woe, and a tale it was. He could fabricate a story out of thin air, and you would believe every word of it. Next, it was Dad's turn to argue his version of life with Robin. Robin won that round. The doctor told my dad he was the one in need of help, not Robin!

When all three of them walked back into the house that afternoon, my heart sank. We were all praying to have a bit of a reprieve from Robin and his manic behaviors; we were all stressed to the breaking point—how much more could we take? I for one craved some sort of normalcy in our home. Dad walked in the front door and headed directly for the liquor cabinet, drank a shot of whiskey, and cried. Helpless—he felt helpless and frustrated and angry and sad, for he could not find a way to help his broken son. There were no easy solutions or answers and no support from the medical world nor the government that had sent Robin off to war (some things never change). Dad dealt with his own guilt for having signed the papers for Robin to enlist; Robin would have turned eighteen in a few months anyway and joined without Dad's permission, but it weighed heavy on Dad's heart.

When I was sixteen Robin married his first wife, Linda, high on heroin. The marriage was filled with emotional highs and lows brought on by the drugs, dysfunction, and nightmares from Robin's time in Vietnam. He was in and out of mental hospitals several times for overdosing on pain meds and trying to commit suicide. Even though I was eight years younger than Robin, we hung with the same crowd of people, attended the same parties, and patronized the same drinking establishments. Drinking age at the time was eighteen, but I was in the bars long before my eighteenth birthday as they never carded anyone in those days. Robin and I were often together, partying and drinking. Friends were a little leery and afraid of Robin as he always carried a gun and his mental state was a bit precarious, to say the least. And while he was still my big brother, our relationship had flipped; I had become his protector when things became volatile and unbalanced. I was the person he reached out to in his darkest moments.

One summer afternoon in 1972, I received a phone call from the police; Robin was sitting in a motel room with a gun to his head. Someone needed to come. My parents were working, so I called a friend to give me a ride to the motel. Once there I was able to calm Robin down enough to get him to the hospital. This would not be the last time I received a phone call from him on the verge of ending it all.

At times during the first part of the 1970s, life appeared somewhat normal and sane and not always chaotic. Robin and Linda had two children, and I loved spending time at their house. We would smoke a little pot and have wonderful discussions about our transitioning world. One evening while I was visiting them, we engaged in a fascinating discussion about the ideology of white and black magic. Linda had dabbled in Wiccan practices, and we had a provocative conversation about supernatural powers and rituals and what can transpire when you evoke these powers. Linda advised me to invoke the name of Jesus Christ for protection if I ever felt threatened or scared by any unseen energies, or so-called spirits.

Well, lo and behold, that night as I lay sleeping soundly in my bed at home, I was suddenly awoken by a ball of bright-yellow light seemingly hanging at the foot of my bed. I sat straight up and stared at this unimaginable light the size of a dinner plate; I didn't know what in the hell it was or what was happening. It slowly faded away. I laid back down and went back to sleep, only to be awoken a second time with the same bright light hanging above my dresser. Needless to say I invoked the name of Jesus Christ (probably with a "what the fuck!") and turned on the lamp, never falling back to sleep that night. This was not a dream, nor was I high; it was one of the most real things that has ever happened to me. In all honesty I can say I was never really frightened of that light; it felt like a good and positive energy force. The incident was imbedded in my memory, and I knew that that light was somehow my guide—my unseen protector and the angel on my shoulder that would be with me throughout my life. It would not be until many years later that I would start communicating with guides and unseen energies, often at Grateful Dead shows and then during meditation.

In 1973 I graduated from high school; I was seventeen years old and had not a clue of what to do with myself. My friends and I spent many a night in Chicago attending concerts. My best friend, Terry, otherwise known as Ratso, would pick me up at home, and my mom would say, "Now you take care of her; don't lose her in the city." She always trusted me if I was with Terry; little did she know when I got in the back seat of the car, Ratso would say, "Start rollin', Mousey" (my nickname), and I would roll all the joints needed for the night of debauchery. Life was a party; there were all of the aforementioned drugs (the Panama Red pot, Quaaludes, speed, and more), and being a good Catholic girl, like in Frank Zappa's song "Catholic Girls," there was sex and rock and roll.

My music tastes continued to evolve. I loved the hard-rock music of Jim Morrison and the Doors, Deep Purple, Pink Floyd, Led Zeppelin, the Rolling Stones, and Elton John and the country-rock music of the Band, the Eagles, the Marshall Tucker Band, Jackson Brown, and the Allman Brothers. I saw several of these groups when they toured in Chicago.

I never got caught up in the disco sound of the late 1970s or the punk, grunge, or alternative-rock music of the 1980s. I do, however, have tremendous respect and appreciation for all musicians and artists. One has to recognize and respect the enormous talent that emerged out of that time period. No one can deny Michael Jackson's unequivocal charisma and musical abilities, for example. He was much more than a musician; he was a showman. His death was another tragic loss of great talent. There was the enormous talent of singers and songwriters such as the Bee Gees and Donna Summer and, in later years, bands like Nirvana, all offering their own interpretation of life through their music. The list could go on. Personally I stuck with the counterculture of the 1960s and 1970s and all the long-haired hippies and freaks of my generation. They fit my criteria.

Through music I found comfort in my life—a sense of belonging to my world. Music became my religion and my escape. I was drawn in by the poetic lyrics. I could relate to the messages and the thought-provoking stories in the songs being sung by Joni Mitchell and Bob Dylan. In my heart, though, I was still lost and searching for something. There was an emptiness lingering deep inside, waiting to be filled.

Chapter 5
FILLING THE VOID

I think we, the Deadheads, all had an unfulfilled space in our lives, and we did not realize we were searching for something real and tangible to fill that void—to help us open our hearts and our minds to the world of feeling and vibration—until we discovered the music of the Grateful Dead.

All Deadheads have a story of when the bus cruised by, we jumped on, and the unimaginable journey began. Not in our wildest dreams did we realize how this adventure would evolve and expand into a fifty-year journey. It is hard for me to remember the exact dates of when things transpired as I did not realize that, forty years after listening to my first Grateful Dead album, I was going to be writing about this adventure. Who knew? But I clearly remember being turned on to *Workingman's Dead*, which was released in the spring of 1970 (although it was probably closer to 1972 when I first heard the album). Ratso was living in a place we called "the lodge," a house down on the banks of the Fox River in North Aurora, Illinois. I was a senior in high school, and the lodge was a party house where we would hang out, smoke pot, and listen to music. One day Ratso said to me, "Mousey, I have a new album for you; you're going to love these guys." He put the album on and handed me its cover. With "Uncle John's Band" wailing out of the speakers and that picture of those long-haired hippie boys on the front cover—especially the cute one, Bobby Weir—I was hooked. I knew this music and sound was something magical and special from the very beginning.

Chapter 6
THE SONG OF LIFE

Oh, how music spoke to me that day. The lyrics of the songs touched a chord deep inside my being. Jerry's guitar licks lit a spark in me, and his soft, soulful voice was taking me home: home to a place I had never been before, to the feelings and emotions of my heart. The music took me out of my head and into a vortex of the unknown, where I could then, as I still do today, submerge myself in the elusive moment of now. And although it would be seven years before I actually attended a live concert, I bought and listened to all of the early Grateful Dead albums and was well on my way to becoming a Deadhead.

In 1976, three years after graduating high school, accomplishing nothing, and going nowhere fast, I decided maybe I should try college. My sister had just graduated from high school and decided to join me, so we packed our bags and moved to Champaign-Urbana in southern Illinois. I attended Parkland College, where I studied graphic arts, and Cindy enrolled in an assistant nursing program at the local hospital. We attended school and worked part-time jobs in restaurants, and we partied. The band Asleep at the Wheel played often in a local tavern/restaurant that brought in bands every Friday and Saturday night. We saw groups such as New Riders of the Purple Sage (without any Grateful Dead members), Pure Prairie League, and the Marshall Tucker Band. In the summer of 1978, after I graduated with a two-year degree in graphic arts and Cindy had finished her studies, we headed back home to Aurora.

During my two years at school, my friends had seen the Grateful Dead a number of times, but I had not yet attended a show. The Dead were scheduled to play on July 2, 1978, at Summer Fest in Milwaukee, Wisconsin. I joined Ratso and a few other folks and headed north, excited to finally see my first show. Summer Fest was held at the Milwaukee fairgrounds, which had several different stages set up for a variety of music, and the Grateful Dead were scheduled to play an early afternoon show. Well, it poured rain that day and the show was canceled. (In all of my years of traveling to see the Dead, I only missed one other show I had tickets for; that was the first show of New Year's Run of 1982, due to a blizzard in Denver). I was disappointed but not totally devastated because, having never seen the Grateful Dead live, I had no idea what I had been missing.

Chapter 7
THE BLUEBIRD SKIES OF ARIZONA

After many turbulent years of struggles and dysfunction caused by drug abuse, depression, and what we now call PTSD, Robin had finally found a place where he felt he belonged: the great state of Arizona. There Robin was able to connect with a group of people who accepted him for who he was and who did not judge him for having fought in the Vietnam War.

The years from 1967 through 1976 had been extremely unsettled for Robin and our family. I often tell people that the 1989 movie *Born on the Fourth of July* was a perfect representation of our lives (without the religious overtones). Robin and Linda divorced, and Linda moved with the children to Arkansas to be near her family. Robin left Illinois in the summer of 1976 with a little money in his pocket and a piece of advice from our father: "Get the hell out of Aurora and go find yourself."

Robin did not have much of a choice in this decision. His drug connections had been cut off. Not only had all the doctors in town wised up to his lies and deceptions, but the local drug and gun dealer, Robin's childhood friend, put the word out: "No more drugs of any kind for Robin; you sell to him, you deal with me!" No one was going to cross that line. The trough had run dry. Robin traveled to California and Colorado and eventually found his way to the Arizona desert. There he finally found some peace in the wide, expansive blue skies and the serene quiet of that beautiful desert. And best of all, he wanted to share his newfound home and friends with me.

In the fall of 1978, Robin came to Illinois for a visit and invited me to go back with him to experience and explore his new home as a college-graduation present. He had been living on the outskirts of the Sonoran Desert with a community of people he called "desert rats." I had never traveled west of the Mississippi River. Our family vacations included Wisconsin and one summer when dad took us on a "real" vacation to Washington, DC, and to the seaside in Ocean City, New Jersey. Having been raised in the hanging gray skies of Illinois winters and the heavy, humid air of Illinois summers, I had not realized the sky could be anything but a hazy, pale blue. I was about to discover the meaning of the phrase "bluebird sky" and understand the lyrics in the song "Jack Straw." For the first time, I saw eagles soaring through a cloudless, deep-blue desert sky.

I naively assumed Robin was taking me to a dude ranch where I would encounter wild horses and cowboys singing around a campfire. Ha-ha! He had not really explained these newfound friends, these desert rats, to me or described his living conditions. I had never been out west, so I only knew what I had seen in the 1960s TV westerns like *Bonanza* and the movie *Butch Cassidy and the Sundance Kid*. I had no concept of what to expect.

When we departed the plane in Tucson, about twenty or so hippies were lurking around corners and milling about the airport terminal waiting to greet us. We grabbed our luggage, climbed into our ride (an old tricked-out yellow school bus), and headed out into the dark Arizona night. This became my first experience of gazing up into the glow of the giant Milky Way lingering in the vast black emptiness of the moonless desert sky. I slept restlessly that night in a bunk bed in a cluttered cabin (not the sprawling ranch house I had imagined), my mind fluctuating from wonder to nervousness of what tomorrow might bring.

In the morning light, I discovered the inconceivable beauty of the desert landscape filled with cacti and breathtaking views of the Tucson Mountains. I was in awe. Early that morning someone had started a fire in which to heat large rocks to be place in a tepee called a "sweat lodge," which sat next to a small metal pool filled with cool water for rinsing off in after the sweat. This was definitely not something I had experienced back in the flatlands of Illinois. Robin still teases me that I was the first person to remove my clothing for that first-time sweat, but hey—when in Rome! This began a three-day celebration (for what I cannot recall). I fell in love with the hot desert sun and the eagles that spread their wings and soared above me in the clear blue sky. I felt enormous gratitude for those desert rats that loved my brother and brought him back to some sense of belonging in this precarious world.

I think Robin understood, correctly, that I would never be fulfilled living in Illinois—that I needed to travel beyond the realms of my familiar surroundings. I had wings and needed to fly. I believe that was why he had invited me to Arizona: to liberate my mind and spirit from the clutches of the Illinois mind-set and to discover the possibilities of what could be. He opened the door and gave me a peek of the choices that awaited me. I can never thank him enough for introducing to me the magnificent wonders of our world, something that he had done since I was a small child.

Back in the flatlands of Illinois, life was resuming its natural rhythm. Mom and dad were less stressed now that Robin had seemingly found some inner peace. David was well on his way to becoming a family man and business entrepreneur, and Cindy was pregnant with her first of four beautiful children. So I packed my belongings and headed west, never to look back. It was time to create my own adventures and discover what was waiting for me in the wings of my life.

I moved to Tucson in January of 1979 and lived with Robin and several other people just outside of the city in a trailer/house that was very funky yet very comfortable. We ate vegetarian food and took long hikes in the desert terrain. Leaving behind the chaotic pace of nightly drinking and partying, I was discovering a newer, softer, and more balanced lifestyle and environment. The desert became a healing place for me as well as for Robin. With the help and support of his friends in Arizona, Robin was able to quit heroin and pursue his dream of becoming a national park ranger. This line of work suited him to a T; he could carry a gun and work outdoors under the canopy of the bright blue skies, protecting his beloved Arizona Mountains. He still struggled and fought his demons, but he found solace and peace in Mother Nature and her inspiring gifts of beauty.

In the early summer of 1979, two of my new girlfriends and I decided to escape the stifling Tucson heat and take an extended road trip to the Northwest. We meandered our way through Arizona, stopping to camp under the starry skies of the Flagstaff Mountain forest. In Utah we discovered the massive red walled canyons where we lingered the day away smoking pot and watching the colors explode around us. The sun grew from yellow to orange to red and then sank into the vast unknown. The beauty was awe inspiring. I had never imagined there could be so much openness, so much pure silence; it was truly a magical day and a moment of discovery.

Upon arriving in Portland, Oregon, we discovered the Grateful Dead were playing a concert at the International Raceway, so we decided join the party. It was an afternoon show and a typical Northwest day: the sky was a misty charcoal gray, and raindrops were lightly descending. We strolled into the venue and headed to the front of the stage; my first show, and I was on the rail! The rain continued until the band walked out, and then, like magic the clouds parted, the sun emerged, and the music flowed. The band opened with "Jack Straw," and I was thrilled; finally I was experiencing live the music I had been listening to for years! I danced in front of Bobby throughout the day, and it was probably the only show where I kept my eyes open until the very last note was played. So on June 30, 1979, I was inducted into the family of the Grateful Dead, and "Jack Straw" became my first choice for show opener from then on.

As we slowly found our way back to the car, the sun receded, the clouds re-formed, and the rain softly fell. The enchanted journey began. I had no idea what surprises awaited me or how my life would revolve around the music of Grateful Dead. But I knew in the hidden corners of my mind that I needed and craved this music that spoke to my soul. I could not have imagined the experiences that would eventually unfold and transpire in my life.

Chapter 8
AWAKENING THE HEART

The summer of 1979, I traveled though the lush Oregon forest and landed in the Cascade Mountains of Washington State. I earned a little cash picking apples in the orchards of Lake Chelan and spent my time living in a one-room cabin surrounded by the sweet-smelling fruit. I immersed myself in the freedom that is so often only available to the young before they get caught up in owning lots of possessions or raising families. Being away from Illinois and my family, I was able approach life with a fresh awareness as I let the hardships and heartaches of what had transpired during the 1960s and 1970s fade from my thoughts. My worldviews were expanding, and my spirit was beckoning to grow, learn, and live.

After returning to the Arizona desert from my extended travels, I was ready to experience something new. (My mother had called me her little gypsy—little did she know.) I packed my meager belongings, said goodbye to the desert and my big brother, and headed for the Colorado mountains. I landed in Denver and began working in a restaurant called Rick's Cafe, where I met my future husband Dan, in February of 1981.

From the outside, the prospect of this relationship lasting long term probably appeared unlikely. Dan and I hail from completely different social and economic backgrounds. I was raised in a middle-class Hungarian Catholic family. My dad was a fireman and my mom an office worker. My extended family—my eighteen aunts and uncles and nearly thirty first and second cousins—were a considerable part of my life. I have no childhood memories that do not include my relatives as we were a close-knit group. We lived within four blocks of my dad's siblings, and they were just a part of my daily life. Growing up in the Chicago suburbs, I learned to be tough, a little outspoken, and a bit wild. One might say I hung with a "rough crowd," although it all seemed so normal to me; the craziness was just a part of life. When I was seventeen years old, a good friend died in a drunk-driving accident. Later that year, my boyfriend at the time was arrested for armed robbery of a convenience store—he needed money for drugs—although he did not end up going to jail for any length of time. Dipping back into the memories makes me shutter. It was amazing I made it out of Aurora, Illinois, alive and relatively undamaged. Drugs were prevalent everywhere, and there seemed to be no rules.

Dan, on the other hand, was raised in Denver, Colorado, in a much more affluent and reserved family. He attended camps in the summers and belonged to ski clubs in the winters, and his high school was a boarding school in Monterey, California. I am six years older than Dan and had been around the so-called block a few times; he was just eighteen when we met. Dan was different from the boys I usually dated; he had short hair, a job, and a car. My parents were extremely impressed when they finally met him; their prayers had been answered.

We met while working in the kitchen of Rick's Cafe, where Dan was my supervisor. One day not long after I had begun working there, he invited me to go see the Edgar Winter Group. I found out rather quickly that he was not as innocent as he first appeared; he may have had short hair, but he was a stoner. Dan is six feet four inches tall, and I barely reach the five-foot mark, but we seemed to fit. I am not confident his parents were as enamored with me as mine were with him. I think they wondered what he was doing with this wild child that spoke her mind. Our love of music, particularly the Grateful Dead, became our unwavering connection. There was never a question of doubt or concern about hitting the road to partake in the music. With no children to tend to or corporate jobs to hold us down, we were free travel and dance through life as we pleased.

Dan's parents have a summer cabin located in the foothills outside of Denver. It's a log cabin that was built, along with a dozen other cabins, in the late 1800s. It is nestled at the bottom of a rock canyon and sits about twenty feet back from a meandering, spring-fed creek. It's surrounded by numerous aspen and pine trees and is home to many creatures, from hummingbirds to bears. Lounging on the deck and basking in the warm summer sun is a great way to relax and let the world roll by. While doing just that one weekend in the summer of 1981, we decided to eat some magic mushrooms and take a hike. Dan grabbed a blanket and a little transistor radio (no iPods in those days), and off we went. We hiked to the top of the hill behind the cabin, where we found a clearing, spread the blanket, and turned on the radio.

As we lay up there on a high vista of those craggy rocky mountains watching the fat animal clouds roll by and the crows, ravens, and hawks perform whimsical, swirling dances through the thin mountain air, out of the speaker of that little radio came Jerry singing "Eyes of the World"—unbelievable! Jerry's voice reached deep inside of me. He always had that way of taking me out of the physical realm to a place of wonder and imagination. In that moment of peaceful contentment, I felt as if I were one with the clouds, the birds, and the sweet smell of the dry mountain grasses. I could see clearly how my thoughts determined my perception of the world. How if I looked at life through my inner eyes with love, compassion, and positive thinking, I could let go of fear and anger and just be. The choice of how I perceived and interacted with the world was mine and mine alone.

Jerry had the ability to transform us through the strings of his guitar; that is why Deadheads loved him so much. He could take us to that place of joy—that sacred place inside the heart that is so hard to reach. He was never the spoken leader of the band, but he was our leader, our guru, even though I do not think this was a role he sought. With his twinkling eyes gazing over the rim of his glasses, and his sweet, playful smile, we would follow him through the twists and turns of any song and take that wild ride with him into the magical mysteries of the music. The music floating out of that radio that lazy summer day touched my soul. It may well have been the mushrooms messing with my mind, but I felt an awakening on that amazing afternoon that I could not put a name to. I somehow knew on that wondrous day that Dan and I would be dancing together for many years to come. The cabin became our home base whenever the Grateful Dead, and in later years the group Furthur, played at Red Rocks Amphitheater. We could rock all night and renew our bodies and souls in the peace and tranquility of the mountain energy in the warm afternoons.

Chapter 9
LISTENING TO THE MUSIC

When I felt lost and lonely, I would listen to the music play. The songs would draw me inward, relax me, and ease my fears. I would automatically go to that place of serenity and hope, dreaming of what could be. Life is supposed to feel good; we have the potential to experience joy in our hearts and well-being in our bodies. But we live in a dualist reality with many dramas, and the road is often bumpy. Sadly, we are not taught as children or young adults how to maneuver through the rough times—how to realign ourselves in peace, contentment, or acceptance when life throws us a curveball. We are not taught to take time for ourselves, to go inward and listen to our feelings, and, if we can identify those feelings and emotions, to clearly and safely express them. Most of us are taught we must work hard to succeed in life and be financially secure to be accepted in society. But success is not always measured by how much money you make or how many possessions you acquire. Success, at least to me, is how much happiness and contentment are in your heart—how much gratitude you feel for this precious world we live and play in, and for the family and friends that are by your side through the laughter and the tears. The formula of working hard for the money did not work for me, and the music and the Grateful Dead gave me another road to choose.

Music became my spiritual journey and my path to discovery. The intriguing lyrics and the vibrations that were awakened within my subconscious allowed me to examine and understand my inner self. My perceptions of the songs were mine and mine alone. The music inspired me to look beyond the illusions of the physical world. I have no concept of what the writers (whether it was John Barlow, Robert Hunter, Jerry Garcia, Bob Weir, Phil Lesh, or Brent Mydland) meant the songs to portray; they had their interpretations, and I had mine.

The beauty of the Grateful Dead's music was that you could let yourself spiral into the frequency of the sound and create new paradigms within the context of the songs. The Grateful Dead had a passion for their music; they lived on the road to create music and to tap in to the emotions and vibrations that could only be reached when the songs were played live in front of an audience. Once the song was sung, it belonged to the universe. We made the music together; it was ours as well as theirs.

Chapter 10
THE CIRCUS COMES TO TOWN

When the Grateful Dead came to town, it was as if the circus had arrived, and we were ready for the ride. We gathered together dressed in our colorful costumes, the anticipation of the night growing as we greeted our fellow tribesmen. There were jugglers and music and veggie burritos. There were smiles and laughs, hugs and recognition. There were old hippies, and there were young hippies; some were high, and some were straight. It was a party—the show before the show in the parking lot, also known as Shakedown Street.

The heart of every town gathered to hear the music and to be part of this unconventional family. There we could commune with our fellow tribe members and be with like-minded people who were just trying to get by in our preposterous, fucked-up world. The shows were an escape and a reality check all wound into one. Before the shows we would wander through the parking lot to buy our tie-dyed T-shirts, Grateful Dead bumper stickers, homemade jewelry, beer, or any drug you could imagine. Eccentric, long-haired hippies, throwbacks from the 1960s (where did they get the clothes?), selling whatever wares they had just to make it to the next show. One time I took my sister-in-law, not a Deadhead, to a show and I remember her saying, "If their mothers could see them now." Well, it was true that most of them looked like they had not had a bath in a week or two, and it was hard to imagine what sort of jobs they held down, but some of that was just part of the scene. They were a band of gypsies following the circus. But there was also an unspoken connection that you could not describe with mere words. We were all there for the same reason: for that magical moment inside the stadium when the music began, the energy grew, and the spark inside of us was lit with excitement and joy and oneness. These were moments when we were all connected: the Deadheads and the band, every soul in the place up dancing, singing, and being in that vortex—that vibration of love and connection to five or ten thousand people who were simultaneously strangers and your brothers and sisters. It was the closest I ever felt to my connection with spirit or source or love, whatever label you wish to give it. Later in life I would again find that feeling of connecting to a higher source in the presence of my yoga guru and teacher, B. K. S. Iyengar.

After a few shows of communing and dancing with my tribe, listening to the music and remembering the feelings of belonging to something electrifying and larger than myself, I would go back home to the triviality of my life and deal with the dysfunctions of our world, the government, and people in general. The music would be encapsulated in my cells, and I would immerse myself in that feeling of light that was sparkling deep inside. I would remember what was real and important and what was just part of the illusion of living in the physical world. Our sense of oneness and connection—this intangible feeling of relating to one another on a whole other level of awareness—was a secret that only Deadheads knew and understood. The general public assumed we were a bunch of crazy-ass hippies listening to a bunch of drugged out musicians on a stage; people didn't get it unless they got it. It was intoxicating and impossible explain. We would go back home and rest our weary bodies for a few months until we had enough cash to do it all over again. Oh, the life of a gypsy!

Chapter 11
AND A PARTY IT WAS

Being on the road following the Grateful Dead was a party. It may have been a spiritual adventure on some level, but there were also countless drugs. I had dabbled and consumed many a drug since my high-school days; drugs were just a part of life (as they still are today), and you could choose to partake or not. I started smoking pot back in the day when you could buy a big bag of Panama Red for twenty bucks. I swallowed plenty of downers and uppers, and I dropped acid a few times. But I did not care for the lingering side effects of acid, that feeling of disconnection from your body and the dullness of the mind well after the trip subsided. Now, psilocybin magic mushrooms—that was a different story. I enjoyed that mellow high very much. Mushrooms were more of a natural high, where you could still feel somewhat in control as your mind expanded and the colors melted and swirled together. The mushroom trip didn't last as long as the acid trip, and coming down was slow and easy. Afterward you could eat and go to sleep. The worst part of eating mushrooms was the taste, which I imagine might compare to ripe compost, but once you got through that, it was a very nice trip indeed.

Pot was the first drug that I left by the wayside, mostly because it left me feeling paranoid and lethargic and not in control of my thoughts or my surroundings; being in control of my world was crucial for me. At Thanksgiving of 1981, I went to Illinois to visit my folks and see the Grateful Dead play at the Horizon Theater on December 6. I had tapered back my pot smoking by then, but I took a hit of a joint when it was passed to me because…well, because it was there. I proceeded to get so stoned I stumbled to the bathroom and puked. I missed the first half of the show. I swore I would never smoke again.

I did, however, smoke some opium once. Before I embark on that story, though, I need to describe Red Rocks Amphitheater in Morrison, Colorado. Red Rocks is a geological phenomenon and the only naturally occurring amphitheater in the world. It is an incredible place to experience any musical concert. It is a magical and spiritual place filled with vast amounts of natural history as well as spectacular views. It is surrounded by towering red-rock walls that rise upward from the stage toward the sky on both sides of the seating; when the acoustics and the vibrations bounce off those walls, the music can take you to another place and time and lead you into another dimension.

As I was dancing with closed eyes or watching the moon rise over the towering peaks during a Grateful Dead show at Red Rocks, I would imagine the dinosaurs wandering the acres of prairies and forest. I would picture my fellow Deadheads as clansmen and cave dwellers dancing in a tribal drumming circle around a ritual fire. As my body vibrated to the heart-thumping drumming coming from Billy, Mickey, and their wild array of percussion instruments, I would conjure up an image of them as two peas in a pod. Their drumming was so synchronized that they appeared to be moving as one as they took us out of the realms of sanity and into the dark mysteries of the beginning of time. Behind the stage are what look like ancient snake fossils slithering their way across the rocks. As the lights engage and change on the back wall, the snakes shift into a playful dance, moving with the music. Yes, some of this imagery may have been drug induced, but being in that unique place called Red Rocks could take you on a wild, magical ride to a place you had never been before. It was my favorite venue in which to see the Grateful Dead. In 2003 Willie Nelson surpassed the Grateful Dead for the most shows performed by a single band at Red Rocks; however, that statistic may not have held true had Jerry lived.

DIARY OF A DEADHEAD

In the early years of the 1980s, Red Rocks concert goers would be allowed into the venue in the early afternoon hours, well before the music began. (The powers-that-be soon deduced that this was not a wise idea.) We would stand in line with our coolers of food, our blankets, and whatever booze we could possibly sneak in and commence to party the day away. Before one particular show, we purchased a chunk of opium in the parking lot. I had never smoked opium but was willing to give it a try. Luckily the spirits were looking out for me that day because as we proceeded into the amphitheater, I left the cooler, along with the Jack Daniels, on the side of the path where we had been standing. Yes, I'm blond, but no one else noticed either. That absentminded act turned out to be a blessing in disguise, because had I been drinking Jack Daniels and smoking opium, I probably would have been visiting the medics that evening.

Once the music began to flow and the night grew dark enough that we could smoke without the eyes of security upon us, Dan lit the pipe with the opium and proceeded to pass it around. After a few hits on that pipe, I was quite high and began to feel a little hot and dizzy, so I decided to sit down. Soon I was lying down and attempting to remove a few layers of clothing as I was beginning to sweat profusely. I vaguely heard a friend say, "I ain't never seen her lie down before." Lying there wondering if I was going to pass out, I thought to myself, "If Dan has to call the medics, he is going to kill me! Focus on the music; focus on Jerry's voice," and that saved my sorry soul. Jerry was singing "Crazy Fingers," so I remained lying there with closed eyes and let his sweet, tender voice bring me back around. As I listened to the words and the rhythm of the song, I began to realize that what I was constantly searching for was that feeling of contentment deep inside that I could never fully grasp, even though I kept reaching and trying. Soon I sat back up, and my best buddy and lifelong friend Tim, Ratso's older brother, leaned down and whispered in my ear, "It's just the opium, baby; you'll be all right." With that I stood up and began dancing.

We smoked on that opium pipe for a week, sucking out every delicious morsel of resin! Thank God we did not know where to purchase any more. It was an incredibly surreal high, and I found a great understanding of why people became addicted as it brought about those feelings of peaceful bliss that escape us most of our lives. I did, however, find my inner joy and peace many times listening to the music and dancing with the Grateful Dead. I realized that once that spark of awareness is lit, you begin to discover new understandings of the mysteries of life; you begin to become aware of the higher vibrations of the nonphysical world. Your spirit awakens and you reach for more. That was the only time I ever smoked opium, but I was glad I did.

In the summer of 1985, Dan and I decided to move to California. Dan, having gone to school in California, wanted to return to the West Coast, and of course we would be closer to the Grateful Dead. We found a place to rent in Capitola (a beautiful little coastal town just south of Santa Cruz), settled in, found jobs in restaurants, and began living that laid-back California lifestyle. Only it was not all that laid back. Cocaine was the fashionable drug of the time; everyone was snorting large amounts of it, and we joined right in.

In the nine months we resided in California, we saw the Grateful Dead eleven times. In June of 1986, we went to Berkeley to see the shows at the Greek Theater, a beautiful outdoor amphitheater. During the set break of the first show, Dan and I strolled up into the back area of the theater, searching for some privacy amid the trees in which to have a little snort. Bad idea! Dan reached over to hold a spoonful of cocaine under my nose. I was holding the vial with the cocaine in one hand and its top in the other when I suddenly looked over and saw two cops walking straight toward us. My mind started racing; all I could think was, "Fuck, get rid of it!" I pushed Dan's arm away from me and at the same moment let the vial fly. I was shaking like a leaf; the last thing I wanted to see was the inside of a Berkeley jail cell. I still shake just thinking about it. The cops approached us and asked me to hold out my hands, but all I had was the lid of the vial. They searched all through the undergrowth of the trees for that vial holding the cocaine but, thankfully, were unsuccessful. Several Deadheads were meandering about watching this drama unfold, and I am sure they were rooting for us. I also imagine someone eventually found that vial of cocaine.

That was it for me; I was embarrassed and shaken, and I was done with cocaine. I was not particularly enjoying it any longer anyway. I hated wasting my money on a useless drug that gave you a false sense of being on top of the world for such a short amount of time. That near miss was my wake-up call; it was time to make some changes. I decided I wanted a healthier, mellower lifestyle, one that did not include drugs, and I wanted to go home to Colorado. California was beautiful, lush, and close to the Dead, but it was not where I belonged. I missed my Colorado friends, and I missed the wide open spaces and the clear blue skies of the high Rocky Mountains. This was a major turning point in my relationship with Dan. He wanted to stay in California. I was returning to Colorado, with or without him. He decided to join me.

Chapter 12
DISCOVERING MY DREAMS

The time had come for me to think about my dreams. I was thirty-one years old. What did I want out of life? Where was I going? After the Berkeley shows, we packed a moving van and headed back to Colorado. We had no plan—no idea where we were going to live. We were just letting it ride, allowing the universe take us where it may. We were back in Denver by the first of July of 1986. For the weekend of the Fourth of July, we decided to travel south to Crested Butte, Colorado, to visit some friends.

Crested Butte is a quaint little ski town nestled at the bottom of the East River Valley in Gunnison County, on the western slope of the Continental Divide. It was a summer home for the Ute Native American Indians until the 1860s, when the white explorers arrived and opened the coal and silver mines. After the mines were closed, the town slowly started to dwindle away until a ski area was opened in 1960, and a new era began. In 1986 most of the streets in Crested Butte were still unpaved except for the one and only highway in and out of town and the main downtown street, Elk Avenue. The buildings were old and funky, many of them dating back to the late 1800s, and the town had retained its flavor of an old western mining town.

The morning of the Fourth of July, we bundled up in our warm jackets (it was not all that unusual for it to snow in early July) and headed downtown for the eclectic parade. The parade consisted of old military veterans, men who had once worked in the mines, cattle ranchers who had lived their whole lives in the valley, and the new hippies and society dropouts. It was a festival. There were food booths, music, and dancing in the streets. Everywhere we went folks were friendly and happy to meet us. It felt comfortable, laid back, and inviting, a perfect fit for us! That weekend we found an apartment, found jobs in restaurants, and then headed back to Denver to grab our belongings and relocate to the place that would be our home for the next twenty years.

Crested Butte is now a bustling resort destination, but in the late 1980s it had off seasons, which meant we had built in time off in which to travel to see our favorite band. The winter tourist season began at Thanksgiving and lasted until mid-April; the summer tourist season began in late June and ended around the first of October. Not only was the downtime perfect for us, but the remoteness—being nestled in the serene beauty of the valley floor, separated from the world at large by high mountain peaks—was also what I had been longing for. The quiet softness of the winter snowfalls, the gentle spring rains, and the vibrant colors of the summer wildflowers and fall leaves made you think you were in paradise.

Waking each morning to the exceptional mountain views, the luminous blue sky, and the sweet smell of the clean, clear air, you could not help but feel blessed. No one made much money, and no one really cared. Most folks skied all day in the winter, biked all day in the summer, and worked whatever, and however many, jobs they needed to support their passions. And yes, there were still hard drugs (if you felt so inclined) and plenty of pot to smoke (which almost everyone did). Being outside immersed in nature and enjoying this spectacular paradise and all the adventures it had to offer was what was most important. People treasured their friendships and were passionate and devoted to protecting the land and the environment. Folks worked hard and played harder. Everyone had a dog or two; if you did not know who someone was talking about by name, the speaker would say, "You know his dog, Bongo," and you would recognize the person in question immediately. There was a large contingent of Deadheads in town; even the non-Deadheads at least understood the concept. During the off seasons, people headed to Utah to ride their bikes, to Hawaii to enjoy the warm beach, or to California to see a string of shows.

In May of 1987, we traveled back to California to see the Grateful Dead play in Palo Alto and then at the Laguna Seca Recreation Area in Monterey. Laguna Seca had a huge camping area, and most folks who came for the shows camped. It was one large Shakedown Street. There were food vendors, bathrooms with showers, and music being played everywhere. And, unbeknownst to us, it was the venue for the Grateful Dead's video "Touch of Grey."

The night of the first show, May 9, when Bruce Hornsby and the Range and Ry Cooder opened the evening, the Grateful Dead filmed their video "Touch of Grey." We had returned to our campsite late that evening when we got word that the Dead were coming back out! We joined the flock and returned to the venue. We walked in and found a space just twenty yards in front of the stage. Jerry, Bobby, and Phil came out on stage and informed us that we, the audience, were going to participate in the filming of their new video. The experience was exciting, amusing, and extremely long. The band came out and lip-synced the song, which took several takes; then they brought out marionette skeletons to stand in place of the band members and played the song several more times! This took hours. All the while the crowd was coached with cue cards so we knew when to clap, when to cheer, and when to be quiet. Meanwhile, the fog from the Pacific coastline rolled in as if on cue to create a mystical, eerie backdrop.

The video got significant airplay on MTV and went on to become a top-ten hit. The Grateful Dead had finally achieved the popular commercial success that had eluded them until then. They finally received the recognition they had always deserved, but it came with a price. Gone were the days when you gave away tickets to a show; instead, the concerts were sold out. A couple thousand people would be partying outside of the venues, searching for that miracle ticket or, later, trying to sneak into the show without a ticket. The stadiums had to be larger to accommodate all the new Deadheads who had been turned on to music and the scene.

Everyone suddenly wanted to join the party! With the increase in fans came the increase of security and scrutiny. People were being busted for smoking pot, and there was a considerable police presence at all of the shows. The atmosphere had changed; our secret was revealed: These guys can jam! For the band's part, the music was amazingly tight and powerful. Jerry looked and sounded great and was notably engaging with the audience, and Brent was coming into his own with a much more vocal presence.

On the 1989 album *Built To Last*, the thirteenth and final studio album by the Grateful Dead, Brent had four new songs: "Just a Little Light," "Blow Away," "We Can Run," and "I Will Take You Home" (my personal favorite). Brent had a rough, gravelly voice, and he played his Hammond B-3 organ with fervor and energy. He put his heart and soul into the songs he wailed out, and it was hard not to get caught up in his intensity. He added a rich, bluesy depth and flavor to the music.

August 13, 1987, was the last time the Grateful Dead would play a concert at Red Rocks Amphitheater. I climbed to the top of the amphitheater to listen to the encore, "Knockin' on Heaven's Door." As I danced to the song and looked out over the massive crowd, all on their feet dancing and singing along, tears fell from my eyes. I knew this experience would soon be a fleeting memory. I felt so blessed to be part of this moment, and all the moments past and future, in Grateful Dead history. I felt tremendous love and gratitude for those musicians on that stage, for the years of inspiring music, and for the fascinating realizations that had engulfed and tantalized my psyche throughout the years. I could not imagine my life without the Grateful Dead.

August 16 and 17 of 1987 marked the Harmonic Convergence, the first globally synchronized meditation celebrating the unusual alignment of the planets of our solar system. It happened to coincide with the Grateful Dead's concert in Telluride, Colorado.

I was as excited about seeing the Grateful Dead play in my own backyard (Telluride is only three hours from Crested Butte) as I was for the Harmonic Convergence. In Crested Butte I had joined a group of ladies who got together each week to meditate and discuss spiritual ideas and concepts. One of these ladies was a channel (a medium through which a message is verbally transmitted), and she would channel a group of entities called the Federation of Light. We could ask these nonphysical entities any questions we had, and they would speak through the channel of the changing times. They communicated through the channel about how we, the human race, were moving forward toward our own transformation and evolution. These guides emphasized the importance of staying grounded during the turbulent times that were impending and the significance of spiritual practices such as yoga and meditation. They spoke of the major changes embarking on our spiritual and political realms. We were just beginning our exit from the Piscine Age, a 2,150-year astrological cycle that was dominated by religious and political hierarchy and power, and entering the beginning our transition into the dawn of the Aquarian Age (as the 5th Dimension sang about in 1969).

We are now on the cusp of the Aquarian Age, and the door to our evolution is just beginning to open. The transformation into this new age will still take many years to complete. As a human race, we are moving forward from the dominance of male patriarchal power, where males primarily run religions and governments, to an age of equal balance and power between males and females. Information is now instant, secrets can no longer be concealed, and people all over the planet are waking up and insisting on change. We can see clearly how this is transpiring around our world with the power of the Internet. Everything that the Federation of Light had spoken of back in the late 1980s has come, and is coming, into fruition. Hearts and minds are opening to the flow of new energy and spiritual self-awareness.

Excited as I was for these two coinciding events, the weekend ended up being strange and yet thrilling in an unexpected way. Telluride is a small ski town nestled in a box canyon at the end of a two-lane road. While the scenery is spectacular and breathtaking, the energy surrounding the town can be erratic. It's as if the energy gets caught up in that deep canyon, swirling about with no exit, just bumping up against the canyon walls.

Whenever I have visited Telluride, that energy has always felt the same: capricious and scattered.

Nothing earth-shattering transpired with the Harmonic Convergence. Olatunji and the Drums of Passion opened the shows, and there was a sunrise meditation on Sunday morning celebrating the Harmonic Convergence, but it felt uninspiring. While there were some arousing moments of music, the shows generally felt ambivalent. But coincidently we were staying at the same hotel as the band, and that was exciting. Only a few other Deadheads besides our group of eight were staying at this particular complex. After the first show, we were relaxing by the pool where the hotel had set out a buffet for the band when suddenly Jerry came and joined us as if we were old friends! He sat down with us and drank a soda and smoked a little pot as if it was the most natural thing, like he was just a regular hotel guest hanging out! He was gracious and funny and very much at ease. We conversed with him about music, and he told intriguing, funny stories about his life. He was affable and receptive to our questions and our childlike delight of just being in his presence. It was exhilarating! That weekend I got autographs from Bobby, Mickey, and Brent. What made that weekend so extraordinary was not the birthing of the new age or the even the music but rather getting to meet Jerry and the band. So special!

Chapter 13
A PIECE OF THE PUZZLE

Life in Crested Butte fell into a comfortable series of new beginnings. Deciding that this would be a good place to plant some roots, Dan and I built a timber-frame house in a subdivision just outside of town and close to the ski area. I also discovered yoga in 1987. Yoga became another piece of the puzzle for me. While I enjoyed skiing and biking, they were not my passions as with some folks. I started attending Iyengar yoga classes offered by the local chiropractor and found yet another path to self-discovery. Thus began my studies of the vast ancient teachings of the mystical sages and gurus. I wove this new knowledge into the tapestry of my life.

There were many similarities between yoga and dancing with the Grateful Dead, although neither group of friends could understand this weird connection. Yoga offered me the other half of my spiritual quest; it taught me to go inward, and I learned to breathe. I discovered the connection of body, mind, and spirit. In the Iyengar system of yoga, one works on balance, strength, and alignment; you learn to hold the asanas and discover stillness within the pose. These poses then become meditation in action. Dancing with the Grateful Dead, I moved my body to the flow of the music; with yoga my body learned to find stillness, inner quiet, and peace. Both experiences brought me closer to my authentic self. Practicing yoga, I found a deeper understanding of my inner being. Yoga is an inner sanctuary I can visit each and every day.

It has been, and always will be, my strength when life brings conflicts. When the road gets bumpy, I turn to my yoga practice, my saving grace. So while in my younger years, traveling to see to the Grateful Dead filled an empty place in my life, as I grew older and matured, yoga filled a new space, and I sought the knowledge of the mysteries of this ancient art form.

Chapter 14
EUROPE WITH THE DEAD

In the spring of 1990, the Grateful Dead announced their fall European tour. I was ecstatic! I had been saving for years just so I would have the funds to go to Europe if and when the Grateful Dead decided to take their extended family on their next European vacation. I was determined not to miss out on this adventure. My nest egg had grown to $2,500.

The day to order our tickets arrived, and I was ready. This was back in the day when you had to fill out a three-by-five-inch index card according to very specific instructions—name, address, phone number, the show dates, and number of tickets you wanted—and send it with a money order and self-addressed, stamped return envelope. The Grateful Dead sold tickets for their shows first-come, first-served, so you needed to be organized and precise, which I was. I mailed away for our European tour tickets, and I was extremely proud of myself for having saved that money all those years.

On the morning of July 26, I checked our post-office box, and, lo and behold, there were our tickets. I jumped for joy! That evening at the Gourmet Noodle, where I was the restaurant manager, I was in the bar area conversing excitedly about receiving our tickets when someone walked in with the devastating news that Brent Mydland had overdosed and died that morning. I was in shock and disbelief. The day turned from one of total ecstasy to one of unspeakable sadness. Why did we have to lose another great musician to this much-too-common self-inflicted tragedy?

So much potential and talent was just gone. He was just thirty-seven years old. I assumed the tour would be canceled.

I was the ultimate Brent fan. I loved his songs and the metaphors of the lyrics; I loved his voice and his passion and was so looking forward to seeing him in Europe. The tour did proceed as the Grateful Dead reconfigured and brought in Vince Welnick and Bruce Hornsby to fill that yet-again-empty seat. Brent was the third Grateful Dead keyboard player to die. His last show was on July 23, 1990, in Tinley Park, Illinois, which happened to be the tenth anniversary of the death of Keith Godchaux, the second keyboard player to die. Keith died in a car accident, although at the time he was no longer a member of the Grateful Dead. Ron McKernan, known as Pig Pen, was the Grateful Dead's first keyboard player to die; he passed on March 8, 1973, from Crohn's disease. Vince Welnick continued to be the keyboard player through the Grateful Dead's last concert in 1995. He, too, died, from an apparent suicide on June 2, 2006. Tom Constanten, the Grateful Dead's first keyboard player, and Bruce Hornsby survived the curse of the keyboard chair!

As they say, the show must go on, so we traveled with a plane full of Deadheads to partake in the festivities. Europe was a great adventure filled with many mishaps and much delight.

We traveled the high-speed trains from city to city with a thousand other Deadheads, most of whom also traveled to Amsterdam, twice, even though there were no shows there. It was indeed a trip to visit the hash bars and look at menus that offered twenty or thirty different strains of pot or hash. My traveling companions, Dan and my old childhood friend Tim, thought they had died and gone to heaven. Thankfully, I no longer smoked pot; someone needed to have her wits about her as we spent hours walking, exploring, and getting lost in the fascinating streets of Amsterdam. The phenomenon of a thousand hippies traveling to the only country where drugs could be purchased legally, without the fear of arrest or jail, did not escape the notice of the authorities that ran the trains. It was extremely painful for my traveling companions to leave those drugs behind, but dogs were searching the trains before they ever left the station, and those who did not heed the warnings were truly sorry.

We booked most of our hotels and bed-and-breakfasts before we left the States, so it was a disturbing surprise when we arrived at our quaint little hotel our first night in Berlin and the proprietor informed us, "Sorry, no room." Our train to Berlin was running late that evening, so we had contacted the hotel to say our arrival would be delayed; no one mentioned we didn't have a room reserved. Since East and West Berlin had just officially reunited on October 3, 1990, East Berliners were migrating to West Berlin in droves; there seemed to be no available rooms anywhere! We wandered the streets of Berlin for hours trying to locate the German version of the YMCA, the CVJM, with no luck. Exhausted and hungry, we stopped for a drink and a bite to eat at a local tavern, where I promptly fell asleep in the booth. Hours later, as closing time crept upon us, we learned that the CVJM was just around the corner. Of course, it was closed by then. We slept that night in the parking lot of the CVJM without blankets on the cold hard cement. Awakened by a fine drizzle early the next morning, we gathered our belongings and went in search of coffee and a soft bed. We happened upon an old gambling bar whose window advertised "espresso" and "no CIA or KGB allowed." Perfect! It was like walking into a scene of an old western movie: The air was filled with a smoky, gray haze, and very old men sat around tables playing cards at six in the morning! We looked as strange to them as they did to us, but they served us the strongest espresso I have ever drunk. After our shot of caffeine, we went in search of beds.

There were still many reminders of the war that had been fought in Germany fifty years earlier. We saw half of a brick clock tower still standing (I assume as a remembrance or a memorial) as well as other buildings that showed the scars of the bombings of World War II. While enjoying a beer in a neighborhood German pub on our second evening in Berlin, we met an elderly woman who told us her story of losing her entire family during the war, and we met and became friends with some German folks whose fathers had fought in the war for Hitler. I thought about how strange it was that our fathers might have encountered each other on the battlefield, making me realize that that war was not so far off in the distant past. I wondered about the bloody battles fought in Europe and imagined the small parts my parents played in that tragic war.

The Berlin Wall had actually been torn down in November of 1989, and these newfound friends walked us through the Brandenburg gate to East Berlin (we in turn took them to their first Grateful Dead concert; they loved American music). Walking in the city of East Berlin was like visiting Gotham City in "Batman." The crumbling buildings were a dirty brown, and the streets, the trees, the light, and the atmosphere in general appeared as if a gray fog had physically imbedded itself in and around the city long ago. There was no life force, as if the spirit of the city had died back in 1945 when the Russians and communism had taken control. A powerful sensation engulfed my body; I felt as if I was walking in a time capsule, and the feeling was depressing yet riveting as I realized we were experiencing a very tangible part of history. We were observing firsthand what the repression of freedom and the stifling of a society could do to a people and their country.

After Germany we headed to France, where walking the streets of Paris in the rain felt like home to me. I felt in the depths of my being that I had experienced a past life or two in that old historical city. All of Europe drew me inward to a place of blurry recognition, to a feeling of a strong spiritual connection to the many places we visited. I would get glimpses of past lives lingering at the edge of my consciousness, though my rational mind unable to fully grasp this faded picture. I thought a lot about my parents while I was in Europe. As I had mentioned earlier my dad was a first-generation American, his parents were immigrants from Hungary who came to the United States in the early 1900s, and my mom was born and raised in England. Both served in World War II. My dad was an infantryman in the US Army and was wounded in France; my mom served as a telephone operator for the British army in Edinburgh, Scotland. Maybe these feelings of familiarity came from hearing their fascinating stories as a child. I do not really know. But I felt as if ghosts of days gone by were traveling alongside me through historical streets.

We walked many miles exploring the museums and art galleries of the different countries: the Van Gogh Gallery and Anne Frank's house in Amsterdam (after walking several miles in the wrong direction), and Picasso's home and gallery in France, where I determined Picasso must have indulged in a few mind-altering drugs himself. We wandered the streets and immersed ourselves in the culture, the food, and the warm beer. Dan and Tim called me the engine; they let me be in control of where we went and what we ate, and when I got hungry, they would say, "It's time to feed the engine." It is a good thing that these two men love me (and that they were stoned most of the time) because no one else could have dealt with my Chicago attitude and my need to be in control. I would say to them, "You can argue with me, or you can shut up." It became our standard joke. (After our European trip, I realized I would someday have to examine this need to always be in control. But it took another twenty-three years before I actually looked at this somewhat-flawed personality trait!) The nights were filled with dancing and partying with our fellow tribe members. Some of the venues were small and quaint, while others were large and smoky; Europeans apparently love their cigarettes. Even without Brent the music was tight and compelling. Vince Welnick and Bruce Hornsby brought in their own unique and enthusiastic styles, intertwining with the Grateful Dead as they wove their way through the intricacies of the songs.

London held a wonderful a surprise for me; it is where Dan asked me to marry him. I was quite shocked. Being the little hippie chick that I was, whether we actually married was not of great importance to me after living together for ten years. But the idea started to take hold. After all, we had built a home and a life together, and I was rather confident neither one of us was planning to move on because, well, we fit. Dan and tranquil, laid-back personality and I with my fiery attitude toward everything, balanced each other out. The day he popped the question, November 1, 1990, the Grateful Dead played "Cold Rain and Snow"—how apropos.

Tim glanced toward Dan and shook his head; you could see him thinking, "Yeah, that wife is gonna be trouble!"

Traveling through Europe with the Grateful Dead was a big checkmark off my bucket list; now what? What exhilarating new experience could I manifest in my charmed life?

Chapter 15
THE WHEEL TURNS

Dan and I married on August 10, 1991. The ceremony took place on our back porch with Gothic Mountain and Mount Crested Butte as our backdrop and one hundred friends and family members surrounding us with love and blessings. My brother-in-law Steve played his guitar and sang "I Second That Emotion" and Van Morrison's "Have I Told You Lately." My dad (forever the comedian) gave Dan a stuffed pink pig in payment for taking me off his hands. Samson, our golden retriever, wore a big red bow around his neck and was the official greeter and plate cleaner. It was a spectacular day filled with delicious food and plenty of spirits, laughs, and love. It was a hippie wedding through and through, and I would not have had it any other way.

As we transitioned into the 1990s, I once again began to feel that emotion of emptiness, of some unfulfilled desire lurking in my subconscious. I wanted to have a baby. Being a free spirit and always ready to accept whatever the universe brought my way, I had never used birth control; I would have been thrilled to become pregnant anytime, married or not. I was now thirty-six years old, and my clock was ticking, but in the depths of my heart I knew I would not become pregnant. It was one of those weird things that I just knew. This was neither the first nor the last moment of knowing or intuition that engulfed my psyche. Throughout my life my intuition of future events, big and small, had revealed itself to my consciousness in many strange ways.

Once in Arizona I insisted my brother Robin drive twenty miles out of our way so I could go back home to collect my toothbrush; we were going camping for the weekend and I had forgotten it. Arriving back at the house, we discovered that someone had left a candle burning and that the curtains had just caught fire. It was not like me to be so demanding, especially for a toothbrush, but I just wouldn't let go of my need to return to the house. The house probably would have burned to the ground had I not been so determined! While living in California, it became so common for me to have an inkling of what would happen mere seconds before the event transpired that the sense started to scare me. I would know when a light bulb was going to burn out or would perceive a bumper sticker on a car before I walked past it. I would think of someone right before he or she called. My perception of these minuscule future events was so magnified and constant that I said out loud, "Stop; this has to stop," and it did for many years to come. However, the larger conception and intuition of life's flowing events continued. I eventually learn not to repress those genuine feelings of knowing but rather to take note, listen, and be aware. The times I did ignore my intuition I would think to myself, "I should have paid attention." So I knew a baby was not in the cards for me, but I kept dreaming anyway, hoping to be wrong.

Meanwhile, while I was wishing and hoping, life just rolled on. I came to a fork in the road and needed a change. I was becoming ambivalent about restaurant work; working late evenings was exhausting and uninspiring. One night while enjoying a glass of wine at the bar after a long shift, I stated to a coworker, "I'm done with this; it is time to reinvent myself." And as with most things in my life, when I made an impassioned decision, the universe opened the door for me.

Crested Butte was home to a small health-food store called Mountain Earth that I often frequented. I had been shopping in small, quaint health-food stores since the early 1980s. I love that earthy herb smell that seems to permeate all natural-food stores, even the larger ones of today. Being a good hippie, I wanted pesticide-free and organically grown foods and products that would not harm the environment, but at that time choices were limited.

The morning after making my statement about much-needed change, I inquired about a job at Mountain Earth. A young couple, Dave and Karen, had started the store with much enthusiasm, but actually making a living in this endeavor took determination. They each worked second jobs to make ends meet, and along with engaging in all of the outside activities that they loved—hiking, biking, and skiing—their plates were full. They welcomed me with open arms. The wheels began to turn, and life's circumstances were leading me on a new and exciting adventure.

I was a perfect fit and asset to the store as I love to organize, a talent neither Dave nor Karen exhibited. Soon I had the place sparkling clean and rearranged and business began to increase. Karen became pregnant, and she and Dave began to lose interest in the everyday running of the store; I, on the other hand, was ready to immerse myself in all aspects of the business. In early 1992, they inquired if had I any interest in buying the business; it did not take much for me to say that yes, indeed I did.

The store was located in an old miner's house that had no insulation in the floor. In the winter months, my feet grew so cold that I would run hot water in the claw-foot bathtub in the bathroom and immerse my feet to thaw my frozen toes. The building also came with its own ghost. Many of the old buildings in Crested Butte had old, nonphysical energies, or spirits, and while some were tranquil, others (such as the store's) liked to be mischievous. He would knock products off the shelves, and I often would arrive in the mornings to find boxes, bags, and once even a glass shelf scattered about the store. (I called this energy male because he appeared to me in a dream one night as an old miner.) I called a Wiccan friend, and we performed a ritual asking this spirit to transition to another dimension, or to at least stop being destructive. At the same time our ghost decided to move on, I realized the need for a larger, more efficient space in which to house the store.

My dear yogi friends Gary and Donita, who owned the local Mexican restaurant Donita's Cantina, were embarking on their careers as yoga instructors. They owned the building that housed their restaurant and decided to extend the space to include a yoga studio. They had the brilliant idea to relocate the health-food store underneath the new yoga studio, where it is still located today. Again life presented itself in perfect order, or synchronicity; when you allow life to flow, amazing miracles, big and small, will unfold.

Life was full and happily busy, and although I did not become pregnant with an actual baby, the business became the child that I fostered and encouraged to grow. With the yoga studio located directly above the store, pursuing my yoga studies further was a natural progression for me. So began my journey to become a yoga instructor. I spent an entire year reading and studying nothing but yoga and received my certification in 1993. To receive your certification in the Iyengar system of yoga is a rigorous endeavor; you must be dedicated to the subject and willing to put yourself in front of your peers where you are judged on your knowledge and understanding of this ancient art form. A senior teacher must sponsor you and confirm you are qualified to go before the certification committee to test. Testing includes a written exam on the subject of the sutras, pranayama, and the Sanskrit names and meanings of the asanas, along with evaluations of how you teach and demonstrate your knowledge of the subject in front of the assessors. Talk about stress! The assessors are not shy or apologetic about failing you if they feel you are not prepared to teach with integrity and knowledge. Thankfully, I passed on my first try and became a certified Iyengar yoga instructor.

I now divided my off-season time between traveling to partake in weekend or weeklong yoga workshops and traveling to see the Grateful Dead. At times I had to choose between the two, and although I love yoga with my whole being, I always chose the Grateful Dead. I realized I would have yoga in my life forever; however, I feared the Grateful Dead had an expiration date. I just did not know that that date would reveal itself sooner rather than later.

Chapter 16
THE TIME ARRIVED

On August 9, 1995, Jerry Garcia died of a heart attack while in a rehab center in Northern California; he was fifty-three. My heart shattered into a thousand pieces.

After Jerry's diabetic episode in 1986, when he had been in a coma for six days, he seemed to have bounced back with a renewed energy, as we observed the evening we spent conversing with him in Telluride in 1987. After the European tour and Brent's untimely departure from this world, the band just kept on rolling, their schedule unrelenting and demanding. One would think it would be hard enough to travel and keep that train rolling as a young person, but I imagine continuing that grueling pace as they grew older must have taken its toll on everyone, especially Jerry. There were telltale signs that things were deteriorating with Jerry shortly before his death.

Our last Grateful Dead show was on May 26, 1995, in Seattle, Washington. We traveled to the Northwest to pick up Dan's sister Cini in Oregon, and then headed to his cousin Roo's home in Seattle to hook up and see the shows. The shows were being held at the Memorial Stadium, and, contrary to typical Seattle climate, the weather could not have been more perfect. The music, however, was chaotic. Something was amiss, and it was quite obvious that Jerry was faltering. At times his guitar playing was rousing, but he also forgot many of the words, and his disconnection seemed to rub off on the rest of the band. Throughout the show

Jerry hung his head, rarely looking up at the audience or engaging with the other band members. Our suspicion was that his heroin addiction had once again reared its ugly head and taken hold. The rest of the tour was appropriately named "the tour from hell."

Rumors abounded about that last tour as unfortunate incidents happened at every venue: Two fans fell from the upper tiers of RFK stadium, there were heroin overdoses and a collapsing balcony at a nearby campground, a gate-crashing riot that caused the cancelation of the show the following night, and lightning struck three fans before a show. The parking lot scenes were out of control. The energy had gone awry; this was not the atmosphere that the older, longtime Deadheads desired. After three decades of touring and dedicating their lives to the music that they loved, the Grateful Dead played their last show in Chicago, Illinois, at Soldier Field on July 9, 1995. The encores that evening were "Black Muddy River" and "Box of Rain."

As I was writing this chapter, I listened to the song "Black Muddy River." The lyrics and the melody of the song fit my feelings of Jerry's passing; it seemed to be the perfect song to contemplate Jerry's journey to the other side. It wasn't until I got out the book *DeadBase* VII, that I discovered it had been the last song Jerry sang on July 9th.

How did I know this? Did I intuit this information? Did Jerry whisper it in my ear? Am I connected to nonphysical source energy that guided this information, or was it just coincidence? When I release my resistance and allow my thoughts to flow, am I engaging with my higher self or unseen energies that are helping me to write this story? Is this how great painters paint—in the vortex of allowing inspiration to take hold as their brushes glide across the canvas? Is this how the Grateful Dead did it all those years, becoming one with their instruments as the music lead the band? When we go inward, meditate, quiet the mind, and breathe, do we connect with higher nonphysical vibrations; do we learn to let life flow?

I knew that someday the day would arrive when I would no longer have the Grateful Dead singing me a melody and taking me home. I knew our love would last forever, but this rider would miss those musicians shining their magical light through a cool, misty Colorado evening. And although an era was over, the music would never melt away. I had to grapple with my own feelings of loss; I felt as if something inside me had died right along with Jerry, and it would be years before I could listen to the music without feeling as if my heart was being squeezed by a vise grip.

I was forever grateful for being part of this movement—this thing that could not be explained. I was grateful for all the experiences, the friendships, and the awe-inspiring music. I was grateful that my free spirit had taken me on this wild ride for so many years, but I was most grateful for the Grateful Dead. I loved those guys like brothers. We were part of a large extended family whose spirits had connected in this jungle of time and space. Had we decided before embarking into these bodies to create and partake in this exhilarating game, weaving this tapestry of sound, color, and emotion together as we danced through life? This is a question that I love to ponder; did fate play a part in this drama, or is all of life just random?

This voyage was a roller-coaster ride filled with all the dualistic properties of the third dimension. There were way too many deaths and too much self-destruction, but there was also electrifying love and mind-blowing moments of spirits connecting in the vortex of oneness. We were a rainbow full of colorful sound, and sometimes we opened our psyches with mind-expanding drugs that led us into the unknown mysteries of the universe. The trick was not to get stuck in the kaleidoscope of enticing magic; it was a delicate dance between realities. All of life is a balancing act on a tightrope—a ride on a river that can be smooth and tranquil or rough and wild as we navigate through class-five waves that shake us and wake us to the core of our beings. Life on the road with the Grateful Dead was an unimaginable, marvelous ride. The Grateful Dead were not perfect; they sometimes forgot the words, sang out of key, or got lost in their own dichotomy of the music flowing through their fingers. But that authentic moment of being in the now and accepting whatever came our way is what we loved.

Without shows to look forward to, I immersed myself into my work at the store and into my yoga practice. Yoga gave me the opportunity to continue to travel and to be part of a group of people I could relate to on a spiritual level. Going to workshops was a lot like going to shows, just without the drugs. "What do you think the first pose will be, dog pose? What do you think they'll open with, 'Jack Straw'?" The same pose would be taught a different way on a different day, just as the same song could be played and sung a different way on a different day. The body got worked and the spirit got renewed. There was laughter and love, and the best friends a girl could ever hope to have. Life proceeded onward.

Chapter 17
LIFE WITHOUT THE DEAD

As we flowed our way through the late 1990s and early 2000s, we traveled to see some music. Bobby and Phil continued to tour with their own bands, Ratdog, and Phil and Friends, and eventually the remaining four members of the Grateful Dead formed The Other Ones, and The Dead. But it was not the same. The magic had vanished or was hiding in the wings. Maybe it was the absence of Jerry's energy; maybe I was just growing older and searching for something more concrete; maybe I just missed my old Grateful Dead family. Everyone was forced to shift with Jerry's passing; we had to pick new paths and decide which direction suited our needs. The bands Phish, String Cheese Incident, and Widespread Panic took their places in history as the new jam bands for the new and younger generation of hippies.

Without the Grateful Dead, Dan and I turned to the river to fill the empty days and time with something new and inspiring. Dan took up boating, and we began floating the Gunnison River on hot and lazy summer afternoons. The peace and quiet of the river soothed my soul. As I closed my eyes and let the warm sun bake my body, my ears would tune into the songs of a variety of birds. Dan created his own meditation and connection to nature by stopping and tossing a line into the rippling waters without really caring if he caught a trout or not. Eventually we took to floating the bigger waters of Colorado, even experiencing the mighty waters of the Grand Canyon with cousin Roo and her husband Tim, and his family.

In the grand scheme of things, life on our planet in the early 2000s was perplexing and chaotic, especially in the political realms. Being a liberal, I was hoping to move forward toward a more balanced society where we all prospered. Instead we were heading in the opposite direction. As the world around me whirled more and more quickly, I tried to slow down and grow in my personal life. I was reading and studying the many books being written by enlightened spiritual teachers and attempting to grasp the idea of accepting all the uncertainty manifesting across our planet, instead of living in righteousness and judgment. It appeared to me as if we were blindfolded and walking backward, stuck in preposterous scenarios of dysfunction, hate, and greed.

Life has seasons and flows in cycles, and sometimes life is a wheel that circles around and repeats itself. We as a nation and a human race were on the highway between the dawn of a new era and the dark of night. In many remarkable ways we were progressing, eating healthier and cleaner with organic foods and questioning what was in, or being sprayed on, our food. There was genuine conversation about sustainability and the issues that were affecting our environment and our changing climate. I was forever optimistic that we would gradually move away from our dependence on oil as our only source of energy and start exploring and expediting solar and wind power. I was excited about the new hybrid vehicles and the vehicles like Willie Nelson's tour buses that ran on recycled food-grade oil.

On the other hand, there was the dubious propaganda and talk of war and mushroom clouds (those people should have eaten a few mushrooms)! Those of us who were skeptical—who did not agree with the absurd reasoning to invade a solvent country that had nothing to do with the attacks on 9/11—had no voice. Those who held the purse strings and power were determined to do exactly as they wished. The media moguls and the bought-and-paid-for politicians were too lazy and ambivalent to stand up and fight for the truth. They just fell in line and bought the lies hook, line, and sinker. Where were our liberal leaders? The contrasts were, and still are, dramatic—duality on steroids.

I sat back and watched, shocked and petrified, as this outlandish behavior unfolded; had we come no further as a human race, as a country? I was born into this body, mind, and spirit with a simplistic view of life on our planet; if everyone just loved one another, what an amazing world we could create. But here I was experiencing the same thoughts and fears I had as a little girl back in the 1960s watching the riots and the Vietnam War on our black-and-white TV. Life was moving in a circle; history was repeating itself.

I now sat watching my full-spectrum-color TV as life around our planet and in our country took many twists and turns during the early 2000s and the new era of life after 9/11. Not much had really changed since 1965, at least not politically. We were still being fed the illusions of ideology and being asked to accept and believe our leaders held our best interests in hand. Yeah, right! I understood the need to retaliate against those who attacked us on 9/11. I cried in despair, anger, and fear with the rest of my country; how could this happen, and how could humans hate so much? I did not like the idea of going to war, but I accepted the fact that we were going to engage in a war to confront terrorism. However, I did not buy into the need for a second war with Iraq. The decisions being made to engage in yet another conflict so the few elite running our country could profit were unfathomable to me. Young men and women were being hoodwinked into believing they were being patriotic, fighting the terrorists that attacked us on that horrible day in September of 2001. The facts were skewed; the arguments did not hold water. In reality the war was about oil and the profiteering oilmen that held our highest offices. The 9/11 attacks and the resulting destruction of countries and cultures that did not look like us or follow our belief systems is my generation's World War II. The pain and agony of 9/11 will remain with us throughout our lives; we will forever remember where we were and what we were doing when our lives stopped and changed forever, just as we all remember where we were the day JFK was assassinated.

Through my brother Robin, I have witnessed firsthand what war and the killing of innocent people does to soldiers' psyches, how the memories are imbedded in their bodies, and how their spirits suffer in the agony of cruelties that they have witnessed. Now many more families were doomed to experience the dysfunctions that accompany a soldier home from war. They never return as the same people they were when they left to fight for their country. They never completely heal, if they heal at all. The Grateful Dead's song "Throwing Stones" said it all. "Throwing Stones" was first performed in 1982, and it is still relevant today. The song speaks not only of war but also of the destruction of this bright, shining planet we live on. Money and power versus poverty and the forgotten. We are left on our own to figure out how to proceed on a clear, progressive path.

    I knew I was not alone in my discontent, but what was a girl to do? I focused on my own life, as George Bush asked us to do; let him worry about the wars! I looked inward, trying to find peace and contentment in my own heart. I found spiritual teachers, writers, and speakers to inspire me; my favorites were Deepak Chopra, Eckhart Tolle, and Ester Hicks, who channels the Abraham energies. Yes, channeling still fascinates me, but (I suggest yet again) don't all writers, painters, and musicians get their inspiration from some unseen vortex? As I continue my quest for the answers of the vast mysteries of the unknown, what I have come to understand is that all spiritual teachers basically have the same message: Love is the answer. To love ourselves first and foremost, for if we do not love and forgive ourselves for our own perceived shortcomings, how do we ever forgive and accept others for theirs? We are each born into this physical experience with our own individual path to walk and explore; no one path is the perfect path for all. The lesson I am forever learning is to accept and love myself, as well as others, with all our human flaws and erratic behavior, realizing that we are each where we need to be and we are not in control of what others manifest in their lives. Living in this inspired moment of time and space, releasing, and letting go and letting be is the path I am trying to walk. At times on this path, I feel as though I take one step forward only to slip and slide three steps back. I have taught myself to sit alone in silence, to meditate, to quiet my monkey mind, and to live in present-moment awareness. I used to find profound moments of awareness and oneness dancing with the Dead, closing my eyes to the outside world and letting the music take me to that home inside the heart. Now I search for that place of oneness through yoga, pranayama, and meditation. I'm continually closing my eyes, asking spirit to guide me, and asking source to help me understand this material physical world in which I live. My inner being strives to forgive, and to love and accept everyone exactly where they are.

Chapter 18
THE TIME BETWEEN

We lived and learned and grew upon the mountaintop in Crested Butte for twenty years, and in 2004 Dan and I decided we had had enough of living at nine thousand feet of elevation. Shoveling snow nine months of the year had grown old and lost its appeal. We were ready for longer summers and slightly milder winters, at least in relationship to the amount of snow that accumulated in the yard. Moving thirty miles south to the ranchlands of Gunnison, Colorado, was an alluring concept as we could continue to live in this beautiful valley and be closer to the river that we loved to ride.

In June of 2004, we put our house on the market, and on September 5th we sold it. The day was unbelievably gorgeous and warm, and the trees were shimmering a golden yellow-orange against a background of a deep-cerulean-blue sky. With Mount Crested Butte towering to the east, Whetstone Mountain to the south, Gothic Mountain to the north, and the autumn colors exploding on the hillsides, the day was a bona-fide picture-perfect postcard. I would have bought my house that day! Two years after selling our home, we sold the health-food store to my sister-in-law Cini, and life took another turn.

Gunnison is a cow town and a mixture of contrasts. There are the old-time ranching families and young liberal college students. It is a laid-back community with that small-town feel of Bedford Falls (from my favorite Christmas movie *It's a Wonderful Life*). In early December, regardless of the freezing temperatures, we have the tree-lighting celebration. All the storefronts are decorated in festive fare, and there is music and hot chocolate and mingling with friends and neighbors. The children wait for Santa to be pulled through the streets of town in his horse-driven sleigh to light the gigantic Christmas tree set in the middle of the street. In the summer we have a week of celebrating our ranching history with Cattlemen's Days. The 4-H kids show their prized animals in a parade, and the evenings feature rodeos with real bronco-riding cowboys, a carnival, barbecues, and music in the park. There is hiking, biking, fishing, boating, horseback riding, and sitting on the back porch in June sipping a glass of wine, gazing up toward the brilliant stars in the sky. If you're seeking the excitement of the nightlife other than the stars this is not the place to be.

Being free of the demands of running a business gave me the opportunity to do what I loved to do: teach yoga. I opened a yoga studio in a quaint little space behind the town's naturopathic clinic, and a community of like-minded yogis was formed. And as the universe has a way of always throwing me the unexpected curveball, a baby was to arrive to open my heart to a love that I could not have fathomed.

My mom turned eighty in 2006, and to celebrate her birthday she and I took a trip to her homeland in England and Scotland. My dad died of cancer in May 2002, and Mom was lost and lonely without him; the timing was perfect for us to spend some quality time together exploring and visiting her country. To my delight and surprise, when we returned from our travels my sister's son Eli, who happened to be living in Denver with his future wife, Brittanie, called one morning and said, "Hey, we're having a baby!"

Eli was our surrogate son. He spent many a summer with Dan and me in Crested Butte, tagging along with Dan to the radio station or coming to work with me at the restaurant; he even attended a school semester at the local ski academy. Eli is a talented carpenter and woodworker, and when we bought and remodeled our first home in Gunnison he came and offered his expertise. He fell in love with Colorado as a child, but was growing weary of living in the big city, especially with a child on the way. Upon hearing the news they were expecting I suggested, with great enthusiasm, that they relocate to Gunnison, where that baby could have a surrogate grandma!

Two days before Eli called me with his exciting news, I had a Reiki session (a Japanese technique for stress reduction and healing) with a woman in Gunnison. I had been feeling a little off balance since returning from my trip to England and decided I needed a tune-up. What manifested in that session was an unbelievable sadness at the core of my being—the pain of never giving birth to a child of my own. I thought I had released and accepted these feelings of inadequacy, but lingering in the deep recesses of my heart and soul was anger and sadness. I had all this unconditional love stored inside my heart and no one to give it to. As the session proceeded, the tears flowed down my face; I was angry with every woman who had ever had an abortion, giving up so easily what I could never have. I had not realized until that very moment that I was harboring these feelings; I could not have been more surprised by what transpired in that Reiki session. I went home that afternoon wrung dry, depressed, and empty. Then Eli called, and nine months later the light of my life was born. When I finally released resistance and let go of these buried painful emotions, life brought me what I had always desired; a sweet baby girl named Ryli.

Chapter 19
MY BELOVED FOUR-LEGGED CHILDREN

I would be remiss if I did not write about my beloved pets, especially my little calico kitty named Miss Scarlet Begonia. Anyone who knew her learned to let her walk by, for she was feisty and very different from other girls.

Deadheads love to name their pets, and even some of their children, after Grateful Dead songs or characters in a song. We had Miss Tennessee, a nondescript black-and-white cat that was scared of everything; she would hide behind the bathtub whenever anyone came to visit. People did not believe we even had a cat. Then there was Samson, our golden retriever who was the greeter at our wedding; he love to bark early in the morning hours, waking all the neighbors! Cosmic Charlie and his brother, August West, were our twin black-and-gray tiger-striped cats. Cosmic Charlie returned to the stars one morning before his first birthday when a large predator bird carried him off into the wild blue yonder. We lived in a dangerous environment for house cats, as there were owls, coyotes, mountain lions, and bears, although I do not believe the bears were a real threat. We also had the smartest golden retriever ever, Webster. I know, that's not a Dead name. We planned to name him some obscure Dead name, but my friend Donita, for some unknown reason, kept calling him Webster even before we brought him home, so we thought, "Well, that must be his name," and sure enough it was.

Soon after Cosmic Charlie made his exit from this world, we decided August West needed a companion. I called the vet's office to inquire about any kittens up for adoption, and the staff said, "Yes, please come, we have twelve!" On my way to pick up this new member of our family I thought to myself, shall I name her Sugar Magnolia or Scarlet Begonia? How I knew I was getting a female cat is beyond me because I had decided to pick the first cat that walked up to me, male or female, and that cat happened to be Miss Scarlet Begonia. She was so tiny and so darn cute; oh, how looks can be deceiving! Without hesitation I named her Scarlet Begonia. Scarlet lived up to her name for the sixteen years that she inhabited this world, terrorizing poor August, Samson, and then Webster, and all the mice, voles, birds, and people she encountered. The vet's office had a note on her chart: wear gloves! Scarlet was one tough cookie! Scarlet had a great perception of the world around her and the other creatures that shared her space. One afternoon a neighbor observed her playing and romping in the fields with a young baby fox; that neighbor called Scarlet the Puma. She got cancer on her cute little nose and the doctors had to cut part of it off, but even that did not change her disposition or slow her down. It was hard to employ house sitters when we traveled, for if they were at all afraid of her she ruled them, guarding the door, not letting them enter or leave, or attacking them as they walked by. One of her favorite pastimes was to lick the bowl of Dan's bong. You would have thought that might have mellowed her out, but no.

I loved that silly little cat more than any other animal I have ever mothered. Scarlet and I were connected in spirit; she always knew when I was sad or upset and would come and snuggle with me and send me vibes of love. Scarlet decided it was time to depart this world in October of 2013. She began losing weight and slowing down, although she continued hunting mice up until the day before she could no longer walk. I had just been diagnosed with shingles in my left eye; life was waking and shaking me to the core of my being. Why she chose this time to depart this world is beyond me, because I really did not need the added stress of losing this cat that I loved so dearly. I could not stand to see her suffer one more minute, so we took her to the vet to be put to rest. Scarlet had never been the veterinarian's favorite cat, but he was so tender and sweet, as my left eye was all inflamed and bloodshot and my face red and puffy from crying. We brought Scarlet home and buried her in the yard, where she could continue to oversee and guard the house. Every once in a while, I look out, and a fox will be sitting on her grave.

Chapter 20
COMPLETING THE CIRCLE

Financially blessed through the sale of the store, I was able to be a stay-at-home grandma. My sister, being secure enough in her own self-worth, allowed her first grandchild to call me Grandma, which meant the world to me. Cindy realized how much I had wanted children, and allowing me to experience the love and joy only a grandmother can feel was an exceptional gift of love and understanding that she bestowed upon me. She one-upped me by having twin granddaughters three years later.

In the first few years of Ryli's young life, my heart sang, and I sang to her: "Row, Row, Row Your Boat," along with "Row Jimmy." I rocked her to sleep and then, overwhelmed with love, held her as she slept. I cannot express in mere words how much this tremendous blessing changed and opened my heart. I wanted her world to be utter perfection, and I now understood the fierce protection a parent feels for a child. Ryli changed my life, and I am a more complete person because of her. I also had to learn to let go in many ways, accepting she would need to find her own precarious balance and learn her own lessons of growth. All I could do was try to instill in her a sense of her own self-worth; many of us grow up without being taught that we are worthy of love and true inner happiness. I assume all parents must eventually realize that their children come with their own agenda; you can guide them with positive words and unconditional love, but the road they choose is theirs and theirs alone. I believe we choose the home and parents we are born to; we enter into our physical bodies with a certain knowing and understanding of the experiences we will explore in each incarnation. I also believe the children being born today are much wiser beings than any previous generation, and hopefully they will remember in full consciousness their purpose for arriving in this time and space.

As I discovered a new and all-encompassing love in my life, I also unexpectedly found the completion of the Grateful Dead circle through the incarnation of Bob Weir and Phil Lesh's new band, Furthur.

One evening in the fall of 2009, I was in the living room perusing the channels on the TV. Dan was in the kitchen listing to some music on his computer; it sounded an awful lot like the Grateful Dead. So I inquired from my prone position on the couch, "What show are you listening to? They sound great."

He answered, "It's not the Dead; it's Furthur!"

Really? "Who's the guy that sounds just like Jerry?" I asked.

"That would be John Kadlecik from Dark Star Orchestra." Wow!

Two months later Cousin Roo called from California and said, "Furthur's coming to Colorado; we've got to go see these guys!" Well, OK, I was ready. We had seen Bobby and Phil with the Dead along with Warren Haynes (love, love, love) in Denver the year before; it was a fantastic show, and I was ready for more. Unfortunately for Dan, he had his annual spring fishing trip planned for the weekend of the Furthur shows in Broomfield. Since Dan was usually our chauffer, Cini and I decided to put on our big-girl panties and drive the to the concerts ourselves, praying for no spring snowstorms.

Cini and I met up with Roo and Tim in Broomfield, and the bonus round began. What else could you call this period, the icing on the cake? It was a gift of live Grateful Dead music all wrapped up with a big red bow. It was an exclamation point added to the end of the Grateful Dead. The first set was like a second set in the old Grateful Dead days. They opened that first show with a killer "Viola Lee Blues" and continued with "Estimated Prophet," "Terrapin Station," and "Brown-Eyed Women." When Phil sang the chorus in "Brown-Eyed Women" about the old man getting on, the Deadheads erupted into wild cheers. The second set opened with "The Music Never Stopped," and with that I was back on the bus. I was not only dancing to the music I loved, I was dancing on the soundboard stage.

Derek, who ran the soundboard for Furthur, is friends with Tim, so for every show we attended for the next four years we received passes for the soundboard area or backstage passes to the green room where we could mingle with the band (but of course not Bobby and Phil, who had their own private rooms). Derek was forever gracious in allowing me to stand and dance in the back corner of the soundboard stage (sometimes it's a blessing to only be five feet tall). I tried to be as inconspicuous as possible so as to not lose my prime real estate. Dancing to the music, gazing over the heads of my tribe, I would think to myself, "Wow, unbelievable; how lucky am I?"

It was so damn much fun to be back on the road. The music was tight and strong. The backup singers, Sunshine Becker and Jeff Pehrson, enhanced the vocals and added another layer of dimension to the songs. Bobby and Phil were at their best, clear and unwavering; the music rose to a new level of intensity. Keyboardist Jeff Chimenti played his Hammond B3 with as much fever as all the other keyboardists before him, and Joe Russo was as good as two drummers, the energy he displayed in "Terrapin Station" unequivocal. And if you closed your eyes, you could swear Jerry had reincarnated as John Kadlecik!

It struck me that we had all grown up and grown older in more ways than one, as everyone was relatively sober and straight. As the four years rolled along, the music only got sweeter and tighter. Of course there were those that complained and criticized. Dan would read to me the comments from the Philzone, a website where fans post about the shows, and while most feedback was positive, some of it was mean-spirited. "Bobby forgot the words; he stumbled and fell." Well, haven't we all stumbled and fallen in our lives, having to pick ourselves back up and shake it off and move on? Only we don't do it in front of a live audience that is our extended family. How about saying, "Hey, brother, we've got your back; we still love you!"

You can take the girl out of Chicago, but you cannot take the Chicago out of the girl. I so wanted to express my thoughts to those people who bitched: "Fuck you! You walk in Bobby's shoes for the last fifty years, see how many times you stumble and fall!" Really, these old men did not have to go back out on the road and live out of suitcases and hotel rooms away from their families. They did it for us; they did it for the love of the music. How could you criticize? Bob Weir and Phil Lesh gave their whole lives to the music we all love; you think that was always an easy road? And no, John Kadlecik is not Jerry. Jerry is dead; he's gone and he's not coming back. But I will bet you Jerry is smiling somewhere, happy to know his songs are being sung and his music will live on forever. I will listen to John Kadlecik sing and play his guitar any day. He is an extremely talented musician, and over the four years of playing with Furthur he came into his own. He took the songs that our beloved Jerry wrote and he played and expanded and raised them to a new degree of excellence. I, for one, am extremely grateful, for I never imagined I would be dancing to this incredible music live again. The magic had returned.

Chapter 21
LOST AND SPINNING

I had so much joy in my life. I had my sweet Ryli. I had my mom and my loving husband, and I had Furthur, yet I felt discontentment and loneliness. I do believe menopause played a part in my unraveling emotions; only women who have gone through this natural change of aging hormones can relate to these feelings of having no control over your emotions. Life felt like a circus ride of manic behavior. I felt lost and confused. I wanted to rekindle my spark, my passion, and I was searching yet again for a compass to point the way. I was disconnected not only from myself but also from the world around me. I had so much to be grateful for and yet I was a lost child just drifting away.

I often found myself in turmoil, questioning not only the chaotic world erupting around me but also my own self-worth. Depression seemed to be a subtle, lingering sensation that I could not shake off. I was lonely and sad, and I did not know why. I kept these feelings hidden from those I loved, except my compassionate husband, Dan. As I cried myself to sleep at night, he just held me. He knew I needed to wade through this confusion myself, to figure out how to release this old pain and once again find my balance. He loved me and allowed me to be where I was. When Dan and I were young I thought I had so much to teach him, when in reality it was he who was always teaching me—to be nonjudgmental, to live life in the present moment, and to accept with compassion whatever life was offering.

I realized part of my problem was my lack of control over the things I could not control or change. As I look back in hindsight, I realize that some of my control issues are just part my personality. I like to take charge, I am organized, and I can envision the bigger picture of most situations; this is what gave me the ability to run a business for fourteen years. But I guess I needed to learn the hard way to accept and allow the people I love to walk their own paths, even when the writing was on the wall and the drama could be avoided with a little awareness and contemplation of consequences. This was a hard lesson for me. I also discovered that the other side of this need to control is that I had no control as a child living in the dysfunction of lives torn apart by drugs and the side effects of war. I wanted to control my environment. Hence life would circle back around on me and I would once again encounter lives torn apart by drug abuse and thoughts of suicide caused from depression.

I have a very dear friend who was suffering from clinical depression and, in her situation, a condition that could be controlled with medication, but she was on the verge of committing suicide. Her life was spinning out of control and she was trying to combat her depression with street drugs and alcohol. And I had no control, no way of helping her. I could only stand alone on the sidelines and watch this precious life unravel. When the call came at ten thirty in the evening, I was sound asleep, exhausted from my own depression. My husband woke me, and I rolled groggily from the bed as he handed me the phone to receive this news of pending drama. As I listened to these cries for help, my knees grew weak, my legs collapsed beneath me, and then I was on the floor, my mind screaming, "No!" It was 1972 all over again, my entire being instantly reverting back to the memories of my brother Robin attempting to end his own life as the pain and suffering from the trauma of the Vietnam War was too much for him to bear. Once again I had to pull someone I loved from the clutches of death. Why was I experiencing this situation yet again? What was happening to my life; why did I not have any control of what was transpiring around me? Two days after this episode was when I was diagnosed with shingles in my eye.

Shingles in the eye is not a pretty sight, no pun intended. In the dark hours of a chilly fall night in October of 2013, I woke with a throbbing pain on the left side of my forehead. My inner eyelid was scratching my eyeball like rough sandpaper. My imagination was running wild: Was it a tumor in my brain pulsing against my eye? My heart began pounding in my chest, and my breathing was erratic with fear of the unknown. As the soft morning light emerged, I realized something undesired was rapidly developing behind my eyelid. As eight o'clock slowly rolled around, I called the optometrist and made an appointment for three that afternoon. At one o'clock the brightness of the daylight was unbearable, and the sandpaper had turned to piercing shards of glass. Gingerly cupping my palm over my eye I drove to the doctor's office; I could not wait another two hours.

Stress is a marvelous emotion that can arrive and create havoc in the most stable of lives. If we choose to delve into the madness and examine its causes, it can lead to great realizations and awakenings. I was stressed. The year preceding being diagnosed with shingles had been a chaotic whirlwind of inner turmoil. Depression seemed to linger in the empty spaces of my days, sadness penetrating my heart. I possess many tools in my toolbox of life to release tension and stress: I have yoga, meditation, and a healthy lifestyle. Only I could not grasp the strings to pull myself out of the darkness. Life circled around me, my feet were stuck in the mud, my mind screaming with the need to move forward—something needed to give, and it was me. I needed to face the demons of the past, the ones I thought I had put to rest long ago. The sleeping bear hibernating in the secret places of my being was awakened; it was time to face my fears. It was time to write my story and discover who I was.

Chapter 22
DISCOVERING ME

My body felt like a broken bag of bones. How and why was this happening? It did not take a rocket scientist to figure it out; what was I not seeing, what was I not comprehending? As I conceded to any and all drugs Western medicine could offer to relieve the pain in my eye, I also had to start asking myself the harder questions of why this was happening at this time in my life. I have come to realize over the years that our pain is our messenger. It is never anyone else's fault; there is no one to blame. We are not victims. Life is our mirror, and it was time to examine closely what that mirror was reflecting back to me. The key was I did not feel good about my life. I was not walking my own path or caring for myself. I was not able to reach that place of joy in my heart while I perceived the suffering of others. I was trying desperately to hang on to old ways of being: controlling situations that were not mine to control.

I began to realize that from a very early age I had been a caregiver. Caring for my sister back in 1967 and then for Robin in the early 1970s. I continued to be a caregiver throughout my life. I am the typical wife (how old-fashioned of me). I do all of the cooking and cleaning and the running of the household; of course I would not have it any other way. I dedicated myself to Ryli for the first six years of her life, caring for her while her parents worked until she entered the first grade. Again it was what I wanted. I would not trade one minute of that precious, delightful time with her. When my mom relocated to Gunnison at the age of eighty-five, I dove into my responsibility of caring for her, although she is fiercely independent and did not always appreciate my meddling, and vice versa. We have now found our balance with each other, but it was not an easy task.

I needed to finally, once and for all, realize that I did not need to fix anyone or anything, other than myself. I needed to let go of these past habits, habits that I had formed as a child while trying to control the world around me; it was all OK! It was time for me to say to myself and to the world, "I need to take care of me," and not feel guilty about it.

I made the decision to spend the month of January 2014 in Arizona. The desert has always been a healing place for my soul, and I was in desperate need of healing. Everything that had transpired in the fall of 2013 was the catalyst for writing this book. My stories of dancing with the Grateful Dead and the spiritual journey that ensued through my adventures on the road had been swirling about my mind for many years. It was time to write my story. I had to dig deep to find the confidence to begin this endeavor, but I was determined to do it. So in the cool Arizona mornings I would meditate, do a restorative yoga practice, and write. I discovered through reviewing my personal history where this intense need to control had come from. Understanding my control issues and how, where, and why they had developed in my life helped me to begin to let them go. I began to discover that life heals itself if we stop interfering, and that honoring and respecting the experiences that others choose was my path to healing my own wounds.

Chapter 23
MY DANCING SHOES

Happily, there was one more chapter to experience in my dancing shoes: Furthur's Mexico extravaganza, Paradise Waits. Dan and Cini met up with me in Arizona, and from there we boogied down to the Gulf of Mexico.

Dan had tried for thirty years to convince me to take a vacation to Mexico, but I always said no! If I wanted to spend time on a beach, I wanted it to be in Hawaii, not a third-world country where the police wore machine guns slung over their shoulders. It scared the shit out of me. Only Furthur could get me to cross that border.

The Hard Rock Cafe in Cancun was not exactly a broken palace; it was just an unfinished palace—perfect for Deadheads. The check-in was a total nightmare: hours of chaos while standing in long lines to get your room and maybe a key to that room, but probably not the room you paid for. We were hungry and tired as we waited in these agonizingly long, slow moving lines. They passed out free beer and cocktails to appease the cranky old hippies. But they should have passed out joints and cranked the Grateful Dead through the speakers; then it would have been a party! Some of rooms lacked doorknobs, others did not have working showers, and still others smelled like swamps. It was Mexico, after all, and it was paradise.

The Hard Rock Cafe is a beautiful resort located on the rocky shores of the Gulf of Mexico. There are crystal-clear swimming pools that weave throughout the length of the hotel, along with plenty of poolside bars offering sweet tropical drinks, and restaurants and outdoor grills tantalizing your taste buds with the smells of grilled shrimp and roasted veggies. We spent the days with Roo, Tim, and Cini, and two thousand other Deadheads lounging poolside while basking in the warm sun, sipping cocktails, and listening to Furthur or the Grateful Dead blasting through the hotels speaker. Heaven! One would think we would hear enough of the music we love in the evenings, but we are Deadheads, after all, and we can listen to the music morning, noon, and night! The hotel staff was friendly and accommodating, making up for the lack of doorknobs and showers. As the sun descended in the color of honey, we would meander over to our place near the soundboard and dance the night away, sharing that tasty wine.

Furthur was planning to take a hiatus after the Mexico shows, which made the experience all the more precious. The music rocked. The last night was bittersweet.

They opened the last show with "The Music Never Stopped," and from there continued with all my favorites: "Mountain Song," "I Know You Rider," and "The Golden Road." John belted out an intense and powerful "Morning Dew," and Bobby followed with a "Death Don't Have No Mercy" for the history books; he never sounded better. They ended the second set with "Not Fade Away." And of course the encore was appropriately "Brokedown Palace." As I glanced over at Cini and Roo, I realized they were as overwhelmed with love and emotion as I was; the tears were streaming from our eyes. Oh, what a ride and a long, strange, wonderful adventure it had been.

Chapter 24
MY CUP IS FILLED WITH LOVE

There is no better way to end this tale than to say that I cannot count the number of times my cup was filled with love while dancing with the Grateful Dead.

On August 3, 2012—what would have been Jerry's seventieth birthday—Bob Weir produced a documentary film called *Move Me Brightly*; it was a concert film of Jerry's incredible repertoire of music. Musicians from all spectrums of the musical world joined Bob in performing some of Jerry's most beloved songs. What I realized as I watched these musicians, old and young, famous and unknown to me, was that Jerry had touched the hearts and souls of artists from all generations and all walks of life. He was not only adored by his faithful fans; he was extremely respected by his peers and the many young musicians who were there playing his music, some of whom were just children when he moved beyond this physical realm. There could be no greater honor than to celebrate his birthday through his music. I am sure he was pleased and proud. He was an inspiring human being loved by many, and his presence permeated the event. I believe Jerry is out there somewhere, still smiling that sweet mischievous smile and laughing at the follies of life. I also realized as I watched this celebration and listened to people speaking so highly of him that the music would never evaporate into the fog of the past. The young musicians will keep the songs alive. Jerry, along with Bobby, will be recorded in the history archives as two of the all-time great guitarists and songwriters of their generation. The Grateful Dead will be remembered as musical artist beyond any explanation. The Grateful Dead did it their way as no one else ever had.

EPILOGUE

As I sit here in 2015, I wonder what would have transpired in my life had I remained living in Aurora, Illinois. I wonder if I would have found that rainbow of colorful sound. But I was fortunate enough to have a big brother who loved me and bestowed upon me the opportunity to explore this big, bright, beautiful world and all of its delights. I had parents who instilled in me enough self-confidence and trust that I could walk and dance and discover my own path and determine my own destiny. And I had the Grateful Dead to sing me a song and show me a different home. The Grateful Dead were storytellers; my life danced around those tales told and sung on that shining road.

I am blessed in life and in love. As I grow and figure out the answers to life's challenges, the questions change, and I am given another opportunity to go inward and discover a new and deeper understanding of myself all over again. I have received all I have ever desired, and in my darkest moments, I have awakened to life and the beauty that surrounds me.

Telling this story was a journey into my past, a journey that led me to examine the events and feelings that surrounded those events that I had hidden in the back corners of my mind. At times those memories were very painful, but the writing process helped me let go of the stored-up emotions. Everyone has a story; our pasts shape who we are today, and understanding and accepting the past can lead us down the road to forgiveness and happiness. I could not have started nor continued this incredible project without the help and loving supportive of many family and friends.

ACKNOWLGEMENTS

Writing this manuscript was the first step in caring for myself. In Arizona, after the Furthur shows in Mexico, I mentioned to Roo the idea about writing this book, and she said, "Go for it!" Then I made her read the first agonizing pages, and she lovingly encouraged me to keep moving forward. Dan's cousin Margie was my second conquest; she said, "More—write more; we want to hear more about your brother Robin." Thank you, you two sweet, strong, and loving women, for being in my life and for your unwavering encouragement.

I knew Robin was a huge influence in my life, but I hadn't quite grasped the full significance of the role he played until I reached back in time. There will never be enough words to tell Robin how much I love him and how grateful I am for his tender, kind spirit. We are kindred souls, and I believe we reincarnated into our family together to love and support each other through all of the chaos. Robin is still part of my life, and he still resides in Arizona with his best friend and loving wife, Toni. He and Toni have a ranch near the foothills of the Chircahua Mountains, and there he is working on a building a safe haven for veterans of our past and present wars. Who better to understand the pain of a soldier returning to society after experiencing the atrocities of war than Robin? His place is called Broken Soldier Ranch, and I hope someday to join him in his selfless endeavor. Thank you, Robin, for giving me your blessing in writing my interpretation of our lives during the 1960s and '70s.

I owe much gratitude and love to my sister-in-law and dear friend Cini, who tirelessly read draft after draft of this manuscript, correcting my horrible grammar and punctuation, and for not laughing too terribly hard as I mixed up my words and metaphors. I explained to her that I was not paying much attention in the seventh grade as my teacher tried to teach me grammar; I was busy looking out the window and daydreaming about someday marrying my favorite rocker of the time, George Harrison.

In the summer of 2014, I bravely signed up for a writers' workshop at our local college. There I proudly handed over my very rough manuscript to professor and author Russell Davis. He and his red pen were brutally honest, and I cannot thank him enough. Along with telling me I needed to take a class in English language and grammar, he gave me the best piece of advice I could have ever asked for: he told me not to tell my story but to "show" my story. He then cleverly asked me how I felt the day Robin left for the army; with that question alone, the floodgates opened, and I clearly understood what he meant. We talked for over an hour as my emotions overwhelmed me. He didn't need to spend this time with me, but his kindness, compassion, and advice were invaluable. There was just something about the way he spoke to me that day—almost as a father would guide a child without crushing her dreams. I guess that is the gift of a true teacher. Those were the best $350 I ever spent! Thank you Professor Russell.

Professor Russell also gave me a manuscript format guide so my manuscript would be in the correct format when I was ready to submit it to a publisher. Well, there was no way in hell I was going to know how to get that task done; my computer skills are worse than my grammar! So I called my friend Stephanie to come to the rescue. Yet another godsend and patient angel. I thanked her profusely and explained that if I had to depend on my loving husband to help me in any way, shape, or form with my computer, we would have ended up in divorce court! You're the best, Steph!

My research skills improved immensely while writing this book. Wikipedia provided the timeline and the missing dates for the many television and musical shows of the 1960s, as well as the dates of historical events. But the best resource for the Grateful Dead concert dates and song list was the book *Deadbase VII*, written by John W. Scott, Mike Dolgushkin, and Stu Nixon. I had wondered for years what the exact date and place of my first show in Portland, Oregon was, and they provided the answer (not to mention all of the other concert venues, dates, and trivial facts). Every Deadhead needs this book!

I also want to thank Stu Nixon and his wife, Robin, whom I met through Roo and Tim during our Furthur years, for attempting to help me gain permission to use some Grateful Dead song lyrics in my book. Stu put me in touch with the right people, and even though they declined to let me use any lyrics, I am grateful. I knew receiving their permission was a long shot, but I thought I needed to try. Writing the manuscript with certain songs in mind actually helped me see more clearly the connection of the music to my life. So again I feel gratitude for the clarity that came from the endeavor. Stu and Robin, I hope to dance with you again one day soon.

Our experiences form who we are and who we become, and my childhood experiences would have been empty and lonely without my sister Cindy by my side. We learned to lean and depend on each other at a very early age, as we continue to do to this day; some bonds can never be broken. If you are lucky, a sister is someone you can freely speak your truth to and someone who understands your quirky ways. Thank you, Cindy, for sharing your life and your children with me, and thank you for always being there. I love you very much.

Although I did not mention my brother David very often in my story, for he would not want me to, I need to thank him for being our rock. Every family needs that one stable person that can take care of business without the emotional fanfare that most of us cling to in our daily dramas, and for us that is David. He is our rock and our stability, and we all turn to him in times of trouble. Not sure how you do it brother, but much love and thanks.

Thanking Mom and Dad for bringing me into this world is a no-brainer. We weren't rolling in money, but we always had what we needed, and most importantly, we always had love in our home. Dad worked two jobs to provide the essentials, and there were always more than enough toys under the tree each year at Christmas. Our home was warm and cozy and filled with comforting smells of home-cooked meals wafting out of our kitchen. As an adult I now understand the immense pressure and heartache that came from Robin's being wounded, but through it all they still loved us. Even with the chaos, my childhood was perfect, as it made me who I am today. Thank you, Mom and Dad for teaching me what "family" means.

Eli and Brittanie, I can't thank you enough for being in my life, for being my family, and for the gift of that sweet little girl named Ryli. I cannot imagine how empty my heart would be without that special love. Ryli, my sweet baby girl, I love you more than words alone can say. I look forward to watching you grow and blossom. I cannot wait to see what miracles you manifest in your life.

My two brothers from a different mother, Tim and Terry, a.k.a. Ratso. How did I get so lucky as to have you in my life since childhood? Ratso, who became my friend in the first grade, who cried at my wedding, and who taught me how to roll joints and turned me on to the Grateful Dead. All the shows we saw together, all the laughs, all the craziness, you were always right next to me. I love you. And Tim, who walked me home from school when I was in the fourth grade, carrying my books the whole way. Tim, who followed me from town to town, hanging his hat wherever I called home; we were meant to walk this earth together, side by side. You never forget my birthday, you listen to me cry, you make me smile, and you're always there. Thanks for sharing Europe, and thanks for being my friend as well as Dan's.

Cini, Roo, and Tim, thanks for sharing that bonus round; as Roo always says, "Furthur was a well-oiled machine!" Tim, you are the man! Thanks for the backstage passes, the soundboard, the wine, and especially for your and your brother Kevin's dry senses of humor and mischievous smiles! Thanks for the ride on the river, and thanks for welcoming us into your family. Furthur might be over, but you can't get rid of us that easily; we still have Bobby and Phil, so we will put on our dancing shoes and see you in California!

And my best yoga buddies, Gary, Donita, and Maria, where would I be without you? You've held me when I cried, made me laugh until the tears ran down my face, gave me shit, told me the truth, and kept me real, true friends! Thanks for watching out for me, for being there in my darkest moments. Gary, thanks for carrying my luggage from Denver to Pune, thanks for your expertise in the subject of yoga, and thanks for pushing and guiding me to be a better yogi. Thanks for putting up with us three girls and our silliness; most men never could or would! Donita and Maria, you are my sisters from a different mother. You are always in my heart, wherever I am, whatever I am doing. We may not see each other as much as we like, but when we do, it's as if no time has passed. I hope we end up in the old yogis' retirement home together so we can continue to make each other laugh all the way to the other side.

I would like to say thank you to my friend and partner in the yoga studio, Lynn. I am so grateful you moved to town and that I found someone who shared my passion for Iyengar yoga. I love your sense of humor and your easy outlook on the dramas of life. Thank you for doing the semi final editing of this manuscript.

My longtime friend Sue did the artwork for the cover of this book back in 1991. The dancing skeletons were screen printed on bags and T-shirts for our wedding. Little did I know I would use those dancing skeletons so many moons later. Thank you!

I would not be where I am today without my partner and best friend, Dan. There are not enough words in the world to tell you how I feel. It takes a special person to love someone and let her be who she is; you have always let me be my own person. You have supported me in my adventures and been by my side through the highs and lows. You are my anchor. Together we loved the music, enjoyed the ride, and danced through life. You are a good papa! I could not have chosen a more perfect partner. Your family became my family; they took me in and eventually understood my Chicago ways. You and I have been blessed in this thing called life. Thank you from the bottom of my heart and the depth of my soul. You are my better half.

Of course, I thank the Grateful Dead. I thank you for the music. In my heart, I do believe we chose to dance on this path together. We reached beyond the illusions of the physical world and delved into the sound of the unseen energy and vibrations of the music. The experience of being a Deadhead is really indescribable, but I hope I painted a picture of the true delight that came through dancing with you on this magical journey.

I would like to thank Mallory and Keela at Ro-Sham-Bo for the design of my wonderful book cover and website.

And thanks to my niece Justine for guiding me through Facebook and social-medias ins and outs.

To all the friends who danced beside me throughout the long and unexplainable trip we called the Grateful Dead—there are too many to name, you know who you are—thank you! What a ride it was!

One day a few years back, when Ryil was just five years old, I drove her to her favorite park in Crested Butte. As we were exiting the car, she was singing the words to, "I Need a Miracle," and I thought to myself, "Yes, the music lives on."

To be continued...July 3rd, 4th, and 5th, 2015, Soldiers Field, Chicago Illinois

AUTHOR BIOGRAPHY

Candace D. Carson is a Deadhead. A hippie since the late 1960s, she was introduced to the Grateful Dead's music in 1972, when she heard their *Workingman's Dead* album. She attended her first show in June 1979 and her last in May 1995, just before Jerry Garcia's death. When she's not listening to the Dead, she works as an Iyengar yoga instructor out of her own studio and also spends time pursuing her photography hobby. Carson lives in Gunnison, Colorado, with her husband. *Diary of a Deadhead* is her first book. You can read more stories and view photos from her Grateful Dead days on her website, www.diaryofadeadhead.com, or visit her Facebook page, Diary of a Deadhead.

Made in the USA
Middletown, DE
21 June 2015